CBS NewsBreak 2

CBSニュースブレイク 2

Nobuhiro Kumai   Stephen Timson

音声ファイルのダウンロード／ストリーミング

CD マーク表示がある箇所は、音声を弊社 HP より無料でダウンロード／ストリーミングすることができます。トップページのバナーをクリックし、書籍検索してください。書籍詳細ページに音声ダウンロードアイコンがございますのでそちらから自習用音声としてご活用ください。

https://www.seibido.co.jp

CBS NewsBreak 2

Copyright © 2015 by Nobuhiro Kumai, Stephen Timson

All rights reserved for Japan.
No part of this book may be reproduced in any form
without permission from Seibido Co., Ltd.

"CBS Broadcasting Inc. has all copyrights and all other rights in and to the English and Japanese language transcripts of the CBS Evening News Stories contained herein. CBS has authorized the use of such material for educational purposes only. Any other use of such material, including any copying or reproduction thereof, is an infringement of copyright and may result in civil liability or criminal prosecution, as provided by law."

はじめに

　このテキストはアメリカの3大ネットワークのひとつ、CBSの看板報道番組"CBS Evening News"の中で取り上げられたニュースを主に収録したものです。この番組では時々刻々と変化する社会情勢や様々な事件などが報道されますが、本テキストではそうした生々しいニュースというよりも、最新のトレンド、健康やライフスタイル、ハイテク、経済、ポップカルチャー、エンターテインメントなどの日常的な話題を取り上げ、今アメリカで実際に何が起こっているのか、何が問題になっているのか、人々の興味関心は何かなどについて紹介します。個性豊かなアンカーやレポーターたちが様々な話題について報告しているため、その内容は英語を外国語として学んでいる学習者にとってもたいへん興味深いものがあります。本テキストでは特に日本人英語学習者にとって身近で親しみやすく、アメリカ人の生活や文化を直接反映しているニュースの中から、できるだけ放映時間の短いコンパクトなニュースを厳選しました。

　このテキストではニュースを付属のDVDで視聴し、映像をヒントにしながらナチュラルスピードの英語を聞いてその内容を理解することが第1の目標となりますが、十分理解したあとでニュースの音声（またはスピードを少し遅くした音声）に合せて「シャドーイング」を行うことによって、英語の音声面の強化をはかることもめざしています。アンカーやレポーターたちは限られた時間内にできるだけ多くの情報を盛り込もうとしているため、1分間に150語から200語程度の速さで話しています。スピードが速いため、英語を外国語として学んでいる学習者がそれと同じように真似てシャドーイングするのにはかなり無理がありますが、本テキストでは最新の話速変換技術を用いて、生の素材を生かしながらそのスピードを少し遅くした音声や動画も併せて提供しています。ニュースに登場する人々の英語には生の感情がそのまま込められていますので、それをくりかえし練習することによって、英語のリスニングの能力を高めるとともに、英語特有の強弱のリズムやイントネーションをぜひ体感してください。また、各ユニットの最後には理解したニュースについて、「あなたならどう思いますか、どうしますか？」というように、問題を自分の立場に置き換えて考える活動が用意されています。多量のインプットに加えていくらかのアウトプットをすることにより、学習した言語項目を使いながら身につけることができるようになっています。ニュースを理解するだけにとどまらず、様々な話題について自ら考え、それを英語で表現できる力をつけていただければ幸いです。

Nobuhiro Kumai & Stephen Timson

CONTENTS

はじめに 3

UNIT 1 *UNIQLO Aims High* 6
ユニクロがめざす高い目標とは 〈Business〉

UNIT 2 *Study Finds How TV Affects Children's Behavior* 12
テレビが子どもたちに及ぼす影響 〈Health/Lifestyle〉

UNIT 3 *Texting & Driving… It Can Wait* 18
危険な運転中のメール 〈Society/Trend〉

UNIT 4 *Students Unwind in Therapy Dog Lounge Ahead of Finals* 24
期末試験前のドッグセラピー 〈Health〉

UNIT 5 *Bringing Clean Water to the World through Charity: Water* 30
世界中にきれいな水を届けるための慈善活動 〈Social Activism〉

UNIT 6 *A Wave of Asian Immigrants* 36
押し寄せるアジアからの移民 〈Society/Trend〉

UNIT 7 *Facebook Envy* 42
フェイスブックを見ると気が滅入る？ 〈Social Media〉

UNIT 8	**Smart Networking Tips** 48
	就職先を見つけるためのヒント 〈Networking/Job Search〉

UNIT 9	**Bringing Manufacturing Back to the U.S. via the Robot** 54
	ロボットでアメリカに製造業を取り戻す 〈Business/Technology〉

UNIT 10	**Manners 101** 60
	有名大学でマナー講座 〈Interpersonal Skills〉

UNIT 11	**Baby Boomers Moving Back to Cities** 66
	団塊の世代、街に戻る 〈Lifestyle/Trend〉

UNIT 12	**Law Students Struggle to Find Work** 72
	法科大学院生の就職難 〈Education/Career〉

UNIT 13	**Carbon Dioxide Making Oceans More Acidic** 78
	二酸化炭素で海洋が酸性に 〈Environment〉

UNIT 14	**"Technovation" Aims to Get More Women in the Tech Workforce** ... 84
	女性のハイテク分野進出をうながすテックコンテスト 〈Gender/Career〉

UNIT 15	**Flipped Classroom is Changing the Way Students Learn** 90
	反転授業で学び方が変わる 〈Education/Trend〉

UNIT 1

UNIQLO Aims High

I Before You Watch

Look at the title and photos and then answer the questions.

1. What do you think the title means?

2. Why is UNIQLO popular? Do you think it can become popular in other countries? Why?

Unit 1 - UNIQLO Aims High

II Word Match

Match each word or phrase with its definition below.

( ) 1. My company hopes to **conquer** new markets abroad.

( ) 2. She is **eager** to start her new job in the sales department.

( ) 3. He got a **glimpse** of the movie star through the car window.

( ) 4. My sister bought a **brand new** hybrid car.

( ) 5. It's cold outside. Take this **scarf** with you.

( ) 6. Nike is one of the world's largest sportswear **retailer**s of sportswear.

( ) 7. UNIQLO's managers created a **lofty** business plan for their new store.

( ) 8. All women's **apparel** is on sale today.

( ) 9. I have no **intention** of going to the meeting in New York next week.

( ) 10. The Beatles' style of singing **revolutionize**d the music industry.

---

a. a person or business that sells goods directly to customers

b. a quick look at someone or something

c. to become successful in a place or situation

d. clothing

e. very good or having a high level and quality

f. very excited and interested

g. to make a big change

h. completely new

i. a plan or idea to do something

j. a piece of cloth that you wear around your neck to keep warm

---

III Getting the Gist (First Viewing) [DVD 02:14]

Watch the news and then choose the right word or phrase in each statement.

1. (No / Few / Many) New Yorkers are interested in the new Japanese clothing store on Fifth Avenue.

2. UNIQLO wants to be the largest clothing company in (North America / the U.S. / the world) in the near future.

Getting into Details (Second Viewing) [DVD 02:14]

Watch or listen to the news again. Fill in the blanks and choose T or F for each statement in the boxes.

be out to ~
～しようと一生懸命である

flagship store
旗艦店（中心的な存在の主力店舗）

Nancy Cordes: Welcome back. Well, despite the tough economy, a clothing store company is out to **conquer** the world. They just opened a huge flagship store here in New York, and they hope to be coming to a neighborhood near you very soon. CBS correspondent, Debbye Turner Bell was there when UNIQLO ₁( ) on Fifth Avenue, here in New York.

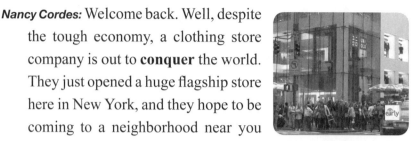

Debbye Turner Bell: The line of **eager** shoppers stretched a full New York City block, waiting to get a **glimpse** of the largest single brand clothing store on Fifth Avenue.

block
（両側を道路で囲まれた）街区

Comprehension Check

1. [T / F] A big clothing store just opened on one of the busiest streets in New York City.
2. [T / F] Many New Yorkers stood in a long line waiting eagerly for the store to open.

Turner Bell: When people walk in, you want them to have what reaction?

Chief Operating Officer
最高業務執行責任者

Yasunobu Kyogoku (Chief Operating Officer, UNIQLO, U.S.): Wow. I ₂( )!

Super Walmart
米国の大手スーパーマーケットチェーンで最大級の面積を持つ店舗

meticulously organized selection of ~
～の商品（品揃え）がきちんと並べられている

Turner Bell: It's called UNIQLO, and the **brand new** flagship store is 89,000 square feet, about the size of a Super Walmart, with 100 fitting rooms, 50 cash registers and a seemingly endless, meticulously organized selection of ₃( ) and **scarves**.

Woman: It's huge. It's… — just there is so much. I walked into another part of the store and I think, there's more?

Man: Hi, welcome to UNIQLO. How are you guys doing today?

> **Comprehension Check**
> 3. [T / F] The new flagship store is smaller than a Super Walmart.
> 4. [T / F] One of the customers is very surprised at how large the store is.

Turner Bell: Right now, the clothing chain has 1,000 stores worldwide. But UNIQLO, owned by the Japanese company Fast Retailing, hopes to increase that fourfold. Simply stated, UNIQLO wants nothing less than to be the largest clothing **retailer** in the world by decade's end.

Kyogoku: Our chairman has said that he would like to be ₄(   ) in sales by the year 2020, 10 billion of which is to be here in the United States.

Turner Bell: A **lofty** goal for an **apparel** company that sold exactly that amount globally last year.

Dana Telsey (Retail Analyst): And when you think of $50 billion, you can think of Best Buy, which is a 50-billion-dollar company, or Home Depot and Lowe's. You don't think of apparel retailers ₅(   ).

Turner Bell: GAP, the largest clothier in the U.S., has recently closed nearly 200 stores, which may be just the opening UNIQLO needs to get a foothold on their way to dominance in the American market.

Kyogoku: It is a statement of our **intention** to **revolutionize** retailing in the United States.

Turner Bell: Debbye Turner Bell, CBS News, New York.

Comprehension Check

5. [T / F] UNIQLO wants to have 4,000 retail stores worldwide by 2020.
6. [T / F] UNIQLO made $10 billion in sales in the U. S. last year.
7. [T / F] A retail analyst thinks that UNIQLO wants to be as big as other large-scale American apparel companies.
8. [T / F] UNIQLO has a big chance to become popular since many GAP stores have closed.

V Summary

Fill in the blanks with the appropriate words in the box below. Then listen and check your answers.

A Japanese clothing store wants to ₁(   ) the world. UNIQLO has opened a brand new flagship store in New York City. American customers are amazed by its ₂(   ) size and the variety of clothing. UNIQLO's ₃(   ) plan is to be the largest clothing retailer in the world by 2020. It aims to have $50 billion in sales ₄(   ), with $10 billion in sales in the U.S. America has large stores like Walmart, Home Depot and Lowe's. However, it is the first time for an ₅(   ) retailer to open such a big store. Since GAP, an American clothing store, has recently ₆(   ) 200 stores, it could be a good opportunity for UNIQLO to get a ₇(   ) in the American market. The company intends to ₈(   ) retailing in the U.S.

lofty	apparel	closed	foothold
revolutionize	globally	huge	conquer

Unit 1 - UNIQLO Aims High

VI. Conversation in Action

🎧 1-05

Put the Japanese statements into English. Then listen to check your answers.

Yuka: Did you check out the ₁_____ on Fifth Avenue?
（新しい衣料店）

Jack: You mean that Japanese retailer? Uh, what's its name?

Yuka: UNIQLO. It's a combination of unique and clothing.

Jack: Yeah, that's it! Not yet. I hear it's pretty good.

Yuka: It's amazing. The store is huge, and they have a wide selection of clothes ₂_____. They say they want to ₃_____
（手頃な値段で）　　　　　　　　　　　　　　　　　　（アメリカ市場を変革する）
_____.

Jack: Wow, that sounds awesome!

Yuka: Why don't we go this weekend? They're having a big sale.

Jack: Great idea! I can't wait!

VII. Critical Thinking

Discuss the following questions with your partner or group. Give reasons to support your opinions.

1. What does "flagship store" mean? Where is UNIQLO's flagship store located in Japan?

2. Do you think UNIQLO's plan will succeed? Why/Why not?

What would you do?

1. You are visiting your American friend in New York. How would you explain UNIQLO to your friend and persuade him/her to shop there?

2. What other Japanese brands/stores do you think would be successful overseas? Why/Why not?

UNIT 2

Study Finds How TV Affects Children's Behavior

I Before You Watch

Look at the title and photos and then answer the questions.

1. What kind of TV programs do you think children like?

2. How do you think TV affects or influences children's behavior?

Unit 2 - Study Finds How TV Affects Children's Behavior

II Word Match

Match each word or phrase with its definition below.

(   ) 1. Grandfather **entertain**ed us with his funny stories and jokes.

(   ) 2. The heavy rain will **affect** traffic conditions in the city.

(   ) 3. Medical **researcher**s say that this new drug is helping many sick people.

(   ) 4. My neighbor is **antisocial**. He doesn't talk to anyone.

(   ) 5. Watch out! My dog is very **aggressive**.

(   ) 6. **Depression** is different from normal sadness. Sometimes therapy is needed.

(   ) 7. Her family is very **concerned about** her safety.

(   ) 8. A **pediatrician** helps sick children.

(   ) 9. He is very good at **imitat**ing famous singers.

---

a. a person who gathers facts and information about something

b. not friendly to other people

c. to perform for an audience or to provide amusement for someone by singing, acting, etc.

d. acting in an angry or violent way

e. to have an influence on someone or something, or to cause a change in someone or something

f. a children's doctor

g. to copy the way someone speaks or acts

h. a feeling of sadness and unhappiness

i. worried about something

III Getting the Gist (First Viewing) [DVD 01:45]

Watch the news and then choose the right word in each statement.

1. New studies suggest that TV could (teach / influence / support) children.

2. Doctors worry that children may imitate (characters / stories / violence) on TV.

IV. Getting into Details (Second Viewing) [DVD 01:45]

Watch or listen to the news again. Fill in the blanks and choose T or F for each statement in the boxes.

have rules in place for~
~するための約束事を設けている

Vinita Nair: Television is a regular part of life at the Walsh house. Kerre and John say they have rules in place for watching, but with six kids..., it isn't ₁(   ) them **entertain**ed.

Kerre: We have TVs in... uh...

John: Every room in the house.

Kerre: Basically every room. And in the cars as well.

Pediatrics
学術雑誌「小児科学」

looked at
調査した

Nair: But two new studies in the journal *Pediatrics* say that TV could **affect** a child's behavior. New Zealand **researcher**s looked at about 1,000 children and found the ₂(   ), the more **antisocial** and **aggressive** they can become.

Dr. Suzanne Kaseta: It also means really more **depression**, more anxiety, more keeping to oneself.

keeping to oneself
人との付き合いを避け、自分の殻に閉じこもること

Comprehension Check
1. [T / F] The Walsh family doesn't have any rules for watching TV.
2. [T / F] Research says a child's behavior could be affected by TV.

Nair: Pediatricians are **concerned** not just **about** how much time kids are spending in front of the TV, but also about ₃(   ) they are watching.

In the second study, U.S. researchers found pre-school age children can **imitate** what they see on TV.

Dr. Kaseta: A lot of children's programming, even though it's children's programming, still shows ₄(   ).

Nair: The American Academy of Pediatrics suggests children older than two should watch less than two hours of TV a day, and that kids younger than two shouldn't watch any TV at all. The Walshes have trained their children so they know ₅(   ).

John: They all shout at the same time. "We're not allowed to watch that!"

TV character: If you wanna be a pirate,…

Nair: They also ₆(   ) during the week… and make sure their children spend most of their time outside…, staying active. Vinita Nair, CBS News, Salisbury Mills, New York.

programming
番組

American Academy of Pediatrics
米国小児科学会

Comprehension Check

3. [T / F] Researchers suggest that small kids may imitate violence they watch on TV.
4. [T / F] The American Academy of Pediatrics says that it's OK for children older than two to watch TV for more than two hours a day.
5. [T / F] The Walsh children are allowed to watch any TV program at any time.

V Summary

Fill in the blanks with the appropriate words in the box below. Then listen and check your answers.

Two new children's studies say that TV could ₁(   ) a child's behavior. They believe children can become ₂(   ) and aggressive by watching a lot of TV. Doctors are not only worried about how much TV children watch, but they are also concerned about what ₃(   ) of TV programs children watch. That's because some children's programs still show a lot of ₄(   ), and children may imitate what they see on TV. Doctors suggest that children over two years old should watch less than ₅(   ) hours of TV a day. They also say kids under two should not watch any TV. The Walsh family makes ₆(   ) about what kind of program their kids can watch. They ₇(   ) TV time on weekdays. They also make sure their children spend most of their time ₈(   ) outside.

kind	affect	antisocial	limit
playing	two	rules	violence

Useful Tip: could は「〜できた」じゃない！?

ニュースの中でレポーターが、TV **could** affect a child's behavior. と言っていましたが、ここでは「〜する可能性がある」とか「〜ということもあり得る」という意味です。下の a) のように、過去を示す語句が明示されている場合は「〜できた」の意味になりますが、b) のような文では、「話し手の確信の度合い（〜かもしれない）」や「可能性（あり得る）」を表します。

a) I **could** swim like a fish when I was a kid. (過去の一貫した能力)
   (子どもの頃は泳ぎがとてもうまかった)

b) It **could** rain this afternoon. You'd better take an umbrella.
   (午後雨が降るかもしれないから、傘を持って行きなさい)

この場合、「今日の午後」というこれから起こる未来について述べているので、could の意味が過去でないことがわかります。

VI. Conversation in Action

Put the Japanese statements into English. Then listen to check your answers.

Amy: No, Peter! They're 1_____ that!
(それ見ちゃいけない〈見るのを許されていない〉のよ)

Peter: Why? It's just anime.

Amy: Some children's programs still 2_____.
(たくさんの暴力〈シーン〉を見せているわ)

Peter: Oh, I didn't think about that.

Amy: Children 3_____.
(彼らがテレビでみたものを真似るのよ)

Peter: 4_____ I think about it, 5_____ I agree. Let's take them outside to play. (そう考えれば考えるほど同感だな)

VII. Critical Thinking

Discuss the following questions with your partner or group. Give reasons to support your opinions.

1. What do doctors say about the effect of TV on young children's behavior? Do you agree?

2. What are pediatricians concerned about?

3. The American Academy of Pediatrics says children need time limits for watching TV. Do you agree?

What would you do?

1. You have a young child. Would you set rules for watching television? What rules would you make? How would your child's age affect your decisions?

2. You are watching TV with your young child when a violent scene appears. What would you do?

UNIT 3

Texting & Driving... It Can Wait

I Before You Watch

Look at the title and photos and then answer the questions.

1. What does the title mean?

2. Why is texting while driving so dangerous?

II Word Match

Match each word or phrase with its definition below.

(　) 1. Thousands of people joined a **campaign** against using nuclear power.
(　) 2. Ken agreed to **take a pledge** to stop smoking.
(　) 3. My cell phone **carrier** has the cheapest and best service plan.
(　) 4. **Statistics** show that teenagers need more sleep than adults.
(　) 5. He won't **get away with** stealing the money. The police will catch him.
(　) 6. Masahiro made **significant** progress during spring training. He will be a starting pitcher for the team.
(　) 7. The new law **ban**s using cell phones in theaters.
(　) 8. The judge **impose**d a heavy punishment on the criminal.
(　) 9. This is her second **arrest** for drunk driving. She will lose her license.
(　) 10. I think we're lost. Let's **pull over** and look at the map.

---

a. legally taking someone, such as a criminal, to jail
b. data that provides information about something
c. very important or having a big effect
d. to make a serious promise or agreement
e. a series of actions for political or social change
f. to avoid being caught or punished for doing something bad
g. to force someone to accept punishment if they break a law
h. a company that provides a special service
i. to say that something cannot be used or done
j. to move a car to the side of the road and stop

III Getting the Gist (First Viewing) [DVD 01:43]

Watch the news and then choose the right word in each statement.

1. (Few / Some / Many) Americans are texting while driving.

2. Texting and driving is the main cause of teen driver (accidents / injuries / deaths).

IV Getting into Details (Second Viewing) [DVD 01:43]

Watch or listen to the news again. Fill in the blanks and choose T or F for each statement in the boxes.

At any given moment
いかなる瞬間でも、いつでも

Ben Tracy: At any given moment, 100,000 Americans are texting while driving. Now a new ad **campaign** asks drivers to ₁( ).

TV ad: Find your reason and **take the pledge** to never text and drive. It can wait.

Tracy: The four largest cell phone **carrier**s are behind this safe-driving campaign. Charlene Lake is a senior vice-president with AT&T.

senior vice-president
上級副社長

AT&T
American
Telephone
and **T**elegraph
Corporation 米国電話電信会社

Charlene Lake: There are **statistics** that prove that ₂( ) and that you cannot just do one quick text and **get away with** it, that there really are **significant** dangers.

Comprehension Check

1. [T / F] A new ad campaign aims to stop drivers from driving while drunk.
2. [T / F] Statistics say that it is unsafe to text while driving.

Tracy: Especially for teenagers. Texting and driving is now the leading cause of teen driver deaths, killing ₃( ) of them each year, more than drunk driving.

Research shows that driving while talking on a cell phone is similar to driving with a .08 blood alcohol content. That's legally drunk. But if you're texting while driving, you're twice as likely to be involved in a crash than if you were drunk driving.

blood alcohol content
血中アルコール濃度

be involved in a crash
衝突事故に巻き込まれる

~~4~~(   ) **ban** text messaging while driving. Only two **impose** jail time for violations. By contrast, almost every drunk driving **arrest** results in time behind bars.

time behind bars
獄中での刑期

Comprehension Check

3. [T / F] Texting while driving is twice as dangerous as drunk driving.
4. [T / F] Many U.S. states still do not ban texting while driving.
5. [T / F] Drivers in all 50 states will go to jail if they are arrested for texting while driving.

Tracy: In Pasadena, California, police **pull**ed **over** this driver today for using a phone. Last month alone, they gave out more than ~~5~~(   ) to drivers for texting or talking on their phones.

Pasadena Police Officer Derek Locklin.

Derek Locklin: This is not just our teenagers. It's adults. It's those parents who are on the phone while their… their children are in the back seat or their teenagers are in the car. So the ~~6~~(   ) is everywhere.

gave out
渡した

Tracy: The cell phone industry's anti-texting campaign begins next week. Ben Tracy, CBS News, Los Angeles.

Comprehension Check

6. [T / F] Last month, only a few drivers got traffic tickets for texting or talking on the phone.
7. [T / F] Some parents are a bad influence on their children because they sometimes talk on the phone or text while driving.

CBS NewsBreak 2

V Summary

Fill in the blanks with the appropriate words in the box below. Then listen and check your answers.

More and more American drivers are texting while driving. Four of the largest cell phone carriers have started a new anti-texting ₁(   ). They want drivers to take a ₂(   ) to stop texting. Statistics prove that texting while driving is not safe. Drivers cannot do a quick text and get ₃(   ) with it. Texting and driving is dangerous, especially for teenagers. It's the main cause of teen driver ₄(   ). It's actually more dangerous than ₅(   ) driving. Thirty-nine of America's 50 states ₆(   ) texting while driving. But only two states impose jail time for lawbreakers. Police ₇(   ) out many tickets to drivers for texting or talking on the phone. They also say that ₈(   ), especially parents, also text and drive. That also has a bad influence on teens.

ban	campaign	pledge	away
deaths	adults	give	drunk

Useful Tip 時には正用法ではないことも？

本文ではレポーターが次のように述べていました。

...you're twice **as likely** to be involved in a crash **than** if you were drunk driving.

「（運転中のメールは）衝突事故に巻きこまれる確率が飲酒運転と比べて2倍になる」という意味ですが、「～の（ ）倍である」と言いたい場合、「（ ）倍 **as ... as** ~ 」が基本の形です。レポーターは最初に twice as likely と言っていますので、その後に as がくるはずですが、比較級の際に用いられる than が使われています。本来であれば下記のどちらかの形式になりますが、実際の生きた英語では、本文のように両方の用法が混じって使われることもあります。

...you're twice **as likely** to be involved in a crash **as** if you were drunk driving.
...you're twice **more** likely to be involved in a crash **than** if you were drunk driving.

VI. Conversation in Action

🎧 1-13

Put the Japanese statements into English. Then listen to check your answers.

Ethan: Did you hear about Yuta? He got pulled over and the ₁_____ _____ !
（警察が彼に違反切符を渡したんだ）

Molly: Seriously? What happened?

Ethan: He was ₂_____ and almost hit a parked car.
（運転中にメールしてたんだよ）

Molly: What? That's so dangerous! What was he thinking?

Ethan: He was ₃_____ for a party, so he tried to send a text.
（遅刻するのが心配だったのさ）

Molly: That's no excuse. Whatever it is, ₄_____. I hope he doesn't do that again!
（それは後回しにできるわ）

VII. Critical Thinking

Discuss the following questions with your partner or group. Give reasons to support your opinions.

1. Why is texting while driving so dangerous?

2. Why do people text and drive even though they know it's dangerous?

3. Is there any penalty for texting and driving in Japan? How about when using a cell phone while driving?

What would you do?

1. You are riding in your friend's car. He/she starts to text while driving. What would you do?

2. What are some things you could do to help people become aware of the dangers of texting while driving?

3. What are some other examples of bad driving habits?

UNIT 4

Students Unwind in Therapy Dog Lounge Ahead of Finals

I Before You Watch

Look at the title and photos and then answer the questions.

1. What does the title mean?

2. Do you know what a therapy dog is?

24

II Word Match

Match each word or phrase with its definition below.

( ) 1. Joyce is studying **psychology** in college. She wants to be a counselor.
( ) 2. How did you **come up with** such a great idea?
( ) 3. Li passed the **finals** for all her spring semester courses.
( ) 4. Daily exercise and eating healthy food helps you **reduce** weight.
( ) 5. Drinking herbal tea makes you **unwind** and feel calm.
( ) 6. Children love to **pet** cats and dogs.
( ) 7. Humor has **heal**ing power because it helps decrease stress.
( ) 8. Jun receives **gratification** from doing volunteer work.
( ) 9. I found my cell phone! What a **relief**!
( ) 10. There was a low **turnout** for the event because of the bad weather.

a. to make someone or something healthy again
b. to make something smaller in size, amount, number, etc.
c. the number of people who attend, or participate in something
d. the state of feeling happy or satisfied
e. to relax and stop thinking about work, problems, etc.
f. a feeling of comfort when something frightening, worrying, or painful has ended or has not happened
g. examinations taken at the end of a semester, or course of study
h. the study of the mind and how it affects behavior
i. to think of something, such as an idea, plan, or suggestion
j. to gently touch a cat, dog, or other animals with your hands

III Getting the Gist (First Viewing) [DVD 01:41]

Watch the news and then choose the right word in each statement.

1. Research in psychology suggests that dogs help to (activate / increase / reduce) people's stress.

2. A special hormone is (reduced / released / received) in the brain while petting a dog, and it makes people feel better.

IV Getting into Details (Second Viewing) [DVD 01:41]

Watch or listen to the news again. Fill in the blanks and choose T or F for each statement in the boxes.

SCC
Southeast
Community
College in Lincoln

Unidentified: Dog kisses on your camera.

Andrea Flores: Dr. Katherine Zupancic is a **psychology** professor at SCC and **came up with** the idea to help students de-stress during **finals**.

Dr. Katherine Zupancic: What we have found from research in psychology is that therapy dogs are often ₁( ) in **reduc**ing stress that people experience.

Flores: Dr. Zupancic and students in the psychology/sociology student group set up a ₂( ) in the student center on campus to help students **unwind**. And, students say it's just what the doctor ordered.

just what the doctor ordered
まさに必要なもの

Comprehension Check

1. [T/F] The psychology professor found a good way to help students feel less stressed during final exams.
2. [T/F] The therapy dog lounge helps students who are afraid of dogs.

Michael McBride (student): I think that, you know, people enjoy dogs. I think that a relaxed dog is kind of nice. You can just sit there and **pet** them and you know, not have to ₃( ).

oxytocin
オキシトシン（脳の疲れを癒し、気分を安定させ、心地よい幸福感をもたらしてくれるホルモン）

Dr. Zupancic: The hormone, oxytocin, that makes us feel good is released. And so it's just a way to sort of ₄( ). It's a way to kind of reduce some of the stress. I mean, sometimes just being able to, to touch an animal, to ₅( ) an animal is... it's very **heal**ing for people.

Comprehension Check

3. [T / F] Oxytocin is a medicine that makes people feel better.
4. [T / F] Touching animals or even being close to animals can reduce people's stress.

Flores: Annelle Straus is a board member for the student group and says the timing for therapy dogs couldn't be better.

Annelle Straus: There's always that instant **gratification**. You just can kind of see that, you know, happy **relief** look on ₆(   ). And we've gotten a really good **turnout** so far. And I think people have been really happy.

board member
役員

look
表情

Flores: With smiles on their faces, I asked students if the dogs offered some relief. The answer was simple.

Do you feel less stressed?

Michael: Yeah.

Comprehension Check

5. [T / F] Annelle says that therapy dogs can make people happy quickly.
6. [T / F] Only a few students have come to the therapy dog lounge so far.

Ⅴ Summary

Fill in the blanks with the appropriate words in the box below. Then listen and check your answers.

A psychology professor ₁(　　　　) up with an idea to help students relax during finals. Research shows that dogs help ₂(　　　　) stress. The professor and her students set up a therapy dog ₃(　　　　) in the student center on campus. They say it's just what the doctor ₄(　　　　). It helps students de-stress and unwind during final exams. Touching and being close to an animal releases ₅(　　　　) that make people feel good. Petting a relaxed dog is very healing for people. They also get instant ₆(　　　　). The therapy lounge is popular. So far, there is a very good ₇(　　　　). Students are happier and less stressed.

turnout	hormones	reduce	ordered
gratification	came	lounge	

Useful Tip

断定的な表現を和らげる kind of, sort of「ちょっと、〜みたいな、〜かなって」

物事を断定的に表現することを避けたい時、kind of や sort of を和らげたい語句の前につけます。本文では次のように使われています。

I think that a relaxed dog is **kind of** nice.（穏やかな犬はちょっといいかなって思う）［形容詞の前］
And so it's just a way to **sort of** feel better.　［動詞の前］
　　　　　（なので、それは気が楽になるみたいな、そんなための方法です）

くだけた会話ではそれぞれを短縮させて kinda や sorta のような発音になることもあります。

I **kinda** like him.（私なにげに彼のこと好きなの）

Unit 4 - Students Unwind in Therapy Dog Lounge Ahead of Finals

VI. Conversation in Action

 1-17

Put the Japanese statements into English. Then listen to check your answers.

Alec: Have you been to the student center? They just opened a Therapy Dog Lounge!

Emma: A what lounge?

Alec: A Therapy Dog Lounge! Students can use dogs to ₁_____ during finals.　（ストレス解消と緊張をほぐすのに役立てるために）

Emma: Seriously? How does it work?

Alec: Simple. Just relax, ₂_____.
You should try it!　（犬をなでて、何も心配しないってこと）

Emma: I think I will! Sounds like ₃_____.
　（まさに必要なもの）

VII. Critical Thinking

Discuss the following questions with your partner or group. Give reasons to support your opinions.

1. Why do you think the psychologists chose dogs for the Therapy Lounge?

2. Do you think other animals can help people relieve stress? What kind? How?

3. Finals are a very stressful time for students. What other things cause stress for students?

What would you do?

1. What would you do to relieve stress before finals?

2. What are three things you could do to make your life less stressful?

UNIT 5

Bringing Clean Water to the World through Charity: Water

I Before You Watch

Look at the title and photos and then answer the questions.

1. What does *Charity: Water* try to do?

2. What do you think "a birthday campaign" is ?

Unit 5 - Bringing Clean Water to the World through Charity: Water

II Word Match

Match each word with its definition below.

(   ) 1. John Lennon's *Imagine* has become the **anthem** of peace-lovers all over the world.

(   ) 2. The United Nations Children's Fund (UNICEF) is an international **charity**.

(   ) 3. We **donate**d our old clothes to the homeless.

(   ) 4. I **post**ed my vacation pictures on my blog.

(   ) 5. The work was **outsource**d to a factory in China.

(   ) 6. The energy **crisis** will have a global effect.

(   ) 7. The water from this **well** is clear and clean.

(   ) 8. The teacher **inspire**d me to study hard and do my best on the test.

a. to give money, food, clothes, etc. in order to help a person or organization

b. a song that has special importance for a particular group of people, an organization, or a country

c. to send away some of a company's work to be done by people outside the company

d. to make someone want to do something or give someone an idea about what to do or create

e. an organization that helps people who are poor, sick, etc.

f. a difficult or dangerous situation

g. to put a message, photo or video online

h. a deep hole in the ground that contains water, oil, or gas

III Getting the Gist (First Viewing) [DVD 01:46]

Watch the news and then choose the right word in each statement.

1. A six-year-old boy (raised / saved / spent) a lot of money to bring clean water to people in Africa.

2. Scott Harrison began a (charity / corporate / public) organization to help build wells through water projects.

IV Getting into Details (Second Viewing) [DVD 01:46]

Watch or listen to the news again. Fill in the blanks and choose T or F for each statement in the boxes.

What about today…? Chris Daughtryの楽曲 What About Nowより **Chris Daughtry** 米国テレビオーディション番組『アメリカンアイドル』出身のロック歌手	**Lory Schwartzman:** What about today…? **Alison Harmelin:** Lory Schwartzman loves to sing Chris Daughtry's popular **anthem** about saving the world. **Lory:** What if our love…? **Harmelin:** And this six-year-old is already doing ₁(　　　　　　　).  **Lory:** Even small kids can do this for other people.
raises money （慈善活動のために）寄付金を募る・集める	**Harmelin:** Lory found out about *Charity: Water*, which raises money to help bring clean water to countries like Ethiopia, Uganda, and India. For his sixth birthday, Lory asked friends to **donate** $6, instead of ₂(　　　　　　　). **Harmelin:** No presents?
Nope Noのくだけた言い方	**Lory:** Nope. **Harmelin:** And you don't miss those presents? **Lory:** Nope. (On YouTube) I'm gonna raise a lot of money. 
An additional ~ さらに〜の	**Harmelin:** After **post**ing a video on YouTube, Lory raised nearly $2,400. An additional 17,000 people have raised $9 million through the ₃(　　　　　　　).

> **Comprehension Check**
>
> 1. [T / F] Lory asked his friends to give money to *Charity: Water* instead of giving him birthday presents.
> 2. [T / F] Lory raised $9 million through the birthday campaign.

Scott Harrison: We've really **outsource**d our fundraising to our supporters.

Harmelin: Scott Harrison gave up being a New York City nightclub promoter to launch *Charity: Water*.

Harrison: I had a huge **crisis** of conscience and realized I was ₄(   ) that I knew.

Harmelin: Now, Harrison and his 50 staffers raise money to build **well**s and purification systems around the world.

Harmelin: In just six years, the charity has provided clean water to more than ₅(   ).

Harrison: Helen in Uganda, who got a water project in her village, and she said for the first time in her life, she felt beautiful, because she had enough water to wash her face and her clothes.

Harmelin: An estimated 800 million people drink dirty water that leads to ₆(   ). Harrison hopes to help 100 million more people in the next 10 years,…

Harrison: Nice to meet you!

Harmelin: …while **inspir**ing the next generation of philanthropists. Alison Harmelin for CBS News, New York.

Comprehension Check

3. [T / F] Scott Harrison started the charity because he realized that he was not a good person.
4. [T / F] *Charity: Water* hopes to help 800 million more people who need clean water in the next decade.

V Summary

Fill in the blanks with the appropriate words in the box below. Then listen and check your answers.

Even small children can do their part to ₁(　　　　) others. Lory, aged 6, asked his friends to ₂(　　　　) $6 to *Charity: Water* instead of giving him presents for his birthday. *Charity: Water* raises money to help bring ₃(　　　　) water to countries such as Ethiopia, Uganda, and India. After posting a ₄(　　　　) on YouTube, Lory raised almost $2,400. Supporters of the birthday campaign raised a total of $9 million. *Charity: Water* was ₅(　　　　) by Scott Harrison. He and his staff ₆(　　　　) fundraising to their supporters. Lory is one of them. *Charity: Water* builds ₇(　　　　) and purification systems around the world. An estimated 800 million people drink dirty water that causes ₈(　　　　) and death. The charity has provided clean water to more than three million people so far. Harrison hopes to help 100 million more people in the next 10 years.

| donate | wells | help | outsource |
| disease | launched | clean | video |

Useful Tip — help の用法

「〜が…するのを助ける、手助けする、手伝う」の意味の help は、help someone (to) do 〜 の形をとりますが、次のように to がよく省略されます。

She **helped me do** my homework today.

本文で、about the *Charity: Water*, which raises money to **help bring** clean water to countries... (…のような国にきれいな水を届けるのを支援するため…) となっているように、**help** の後にすぐ動詞が来て、間に to が入らない形で使われることがよくあります。

その他の例
Green roofs can **help buildings save** energy.
Green roofs can **help save** energy.

VI. Conversation in Action

Put the Japanese statements into English. Then listen to check your answers.

Kana: Our class is having a fundraising event.

Alan: Really? What kind?

Kana: It's a Gospel Concert Lunch! We ₁_____ for tsunami relief in Tohoku.
（資金集めをしたい）

Alan: But I can't sing or cook!

Kana: You don't have to. We ₂_____.
（音楽と食べ物は外部委託したわ）

Can you help with ₃_____?
（動画を投稿したり寄付を集めたりして）

Alan: Sure. It sounds really inspiring. I'll be glad to ₄_____.
（自分のできることをする）

VII. Critical Thinking

Discuss the following questions with your partner or group. Give reasons to support your opinions.

1. Why is having access to clean water so important?

2. The little boy in the news story is just six years old. Do you think it's OK for young children to do this kind of fundraising activity?

3. Have you ever participated in a fundraising campaign or done charity work? Explain what you did and why.

What would you do?

1. Your young son or daughter wants to participate in a fundraising activity for charity. Would you allow him/her to do it? Why/Why not?

2. Your university club would like to volunteer and help a charity. What charity would you choose? Why?

UNIT 6

A Wave of Asian Immigrants

I Before You Watch

Look at the title and photos and then answer the questions.

1. What do you think the word "immigrant" means?

2. Which countries do Asian immigrants come from?

II Word Match

Match each word or phrase with its definition below.

( ) 1. He was **raise**d by his grandparents.
( ) 2. You must pass a special test to become a **naturalized citizen**.
( ) 3. He plans to **market** the new software in Asian countries.
( ) 4. A résumé is a kind of **snapshot** of who you are, what you've done, and what kind of job you want.
( ) 5. My sister is interested in **contemporary** dance.
( ) 6. He aims to **surpass** the world record for ski-jumping.
( ) 7. Women **account for** 70 percent of the sales in this shop.
( ) 8. Many companies cut staff during the **recession**.
( ) 9. Half of all American families have two **wage earner**s.
( ) 10. A wide variety of **ethnic group**s live in London.

> a. to be better or greater than someone or something
> b. to use advertising and other ways to sell a product
> c. someone who receives money for working
> d. to take care of children and help them grow up
> e. to be a particular amount or part of something
> f. someone who was not born in a particular country chooses to become a new citizen of that country
> g. people having the same race, customs, religion, or origin
> h. a period of time when the economy is weak and many people do not have jobs
> i. a quick view or a small amount of information that tells you a little about what someone or something is like
> j. modern; happening, or beginning now

III Getting the Gist (First Viewing) [DVD 02:16]

Watch the news and then choose the right word in each statement.

1. (Few / More / No) immigrants are now coming into the U.S. from Asia.

2. Asian immigrants are (more / less / not) educated than other immigrants and they earn more money.

IV Getting into Details (Second Viewing) [DVD 02:16]

Watch or listen to the news again. Fill in the blanks and choose T or F for each statement in the boxes.

By any measure
どこから見ても、どんな尺度から見ても

Bill Whitaker: By any measure, Jason Yim is an American ₁(   ). How many employees do you have?

Jason Yim: We have just under 70, uh, worldwide. So, we have an office in Shanghai, as well as a small team in Manila, and then this office in West L.A.

Whitaker: He was born in Singapore, **rais**ed in Hong Kong, and came to college at UCLA. After graduating, the 39-year-old **naturalized** U.S. **citizen** started Trigger, a digital marketing agency. His seven-year-old L.A.-based company designs interactive websites, ₂(   ) to **market** Hollywood movies on the Internet and mobile devices.

L.A.-based
ロサンゼルスに本社を置く

Jason: You can see that like, it's just a movie poster. But then when you look at it through the app, Spidey actually comes through it.

Whitaker: This is very cool.

Spidey
スパイダーマンの愛称

Comprehension Check

1. [T / F] Jason was an immigrant from Asia and became a U.S. citizen.
2. [T / F] Jason's company designs digital apps and games to advertise Hollywood movies.

Whitaker: Yim offers a **snapshot** of one of the most dramatic demographic shifts in **contemporary** America. According to the Pew study, Asians are the country's fastest-growing population.

demographic shifts
人口統計学上の変化

Pew study
ピュー研究センター（米国の世論調査機関）による調査

Whitaker: In 2010, more than 430,000 Asians came to the U.S., ₃(   ) of all immigrants. For the first time, Asians **surpass**ed Hispanics, who **accounted for** 31 percent of immigrants. Hispanic immigration is down because of tighter border security and the loss of ₄(   ) in the **recession**.

Most of this wave of Asian immigration comes from six countries — China, India, Vietnam, the Philippines, Korea and Japan. Asians are the ₅(   )  group in the country. Almost half over 25 have college degrees versus 28 percent of the general population. In 2010, they earned 45 percent of all engineering Ph.D.s. They're the country's highest **wage earner**s. Asians have a median annual household income of $66,000. For the general population, it's 49,000. Yim's company earned $5 million last year.

Comprehension Check

3. [T / F] More immigrants from Asia are coming to the U.S. than from any other parts of the world.
4. [T / F] Asian immigrants are less educated and poorer than most Americans.

Whitaker: In a way, you're living the ₆(   ).

Jason: I think so. I think it really is the American Dream that, you know, we can come here, we can do well.

Whitaker: Scott, of course, not all Asian immigrants are success stories, but of all immigrant… of all **ethnic group**s, they are most likely to ₇(   ) across racial lines and live in mixed neighborhoods.

Scott Pelly: Constantly changing America. Bill, thank you.

> **Comprehension Check**
>
> 5. [T / F] Jason is a good example of Asian immigrants who have achieved the American Dream.
> 6. [T / F] Asian immigrants are not mixing well with other ethnic groups.

Summary   1-24

Fill in the blanks with the appropriate words in the box below. Then listen and check your answers.

Jason Yim is a good example of the American ₁(   ). He was born in Singapore. After graduating from UCLA, he became a ₂(   ) U.S. citizen. He started his own business called Trigger and he became very successful. Recently there has been a huge demographic ₃(   ) in the U.S. Asians are becoming America's fastest-growing population while Hispanic immigration is decreasing. One reason is that it is more difficult for Hispanics to cross the ₄(   ) and enter America. Another reason is the changing workforce. Blue ₅(   ) jobs are decreasing because of the recession. Many Asian immigrants have ₆(   ) degrees and earn higher salaries than other Americans. Not all Asians are as successful as Yim. But they are changing America by ₇(   ) people of other races, and living in neighborhoods with different ₈(   ) groups.

naturalized	shift	ethnic	border
Dream	collar	marrying	college

Unit 6 - A Wave of Asian Immigrants

VI. Conversation in Action

🎧 1-25

Put the Japanese statements into English. Then listen to check your answers.

Yuto: I've been ₁_____.
　　　　　　　　　（外国に住もうかなって思ってるんだ）

Lei: Really? Where?

Yuto: The U.S. Did you know Asians are America's ₂_____
　　　_____?　　　　　　（最も急速に増えている民族集団って）

Lei: No. But why do you want to immigrate?

Yuto: I want to live and work there. Maybe someday I'll become a ₃_____
　　　_____. It's my dream.　　　（帰化した市民）

Lei: Oh, like the American Dream! You know, go to the U.S., ₄_____
　　　_____（一生懸命働いて、大きな成功を収めるってことね）
　　　Sounds great! Good luck!

VII. Critical Thinking

Discuss the following questions with your partner or group. Give reasons to support your opinions.

1. The news story gives an example of an American success story. What is an example of a success story in your country?

2. What kind of ethnic groups live in your country? What is the largest ethnic group?

3. Why do you think immigrants come to live in Japan?

What would you do?

1. Would you like to immigrate to another country? Where would you go?

2. Your friend is thinking about living and working abroad. What kind of advice would you give him/her?

UNIT 7

Facebook Envy

I Before You Watch

Look at the title and photos and then answer the questions.

1. Are you using social media like Facebook? Why / Why not?

2. How do you feel when you look at your friends' Facebook pages?

Unit 7 - Facebook Envy

II Word Match

Match each word or phrase with its definition below.

(   ) 1. He watched the winner of the race with **envy**.
(   ) 2. I saw your new **profile** on Facebook. It looks great!
(   ) 3. After traveling around the world, he **end**ed **up** liv**ing** in New York.
(   ) 4. The earthquake caused great **distress** to many people.
(   ) 5. He is **struggl**ing **with** paying his tuition.
(   ) 6. He **play**ed **up** his job description so people would think he is important.
(   ) 7. This plane carries 461 people **exclud**ing the crew and cabin attendants.
(   ) 8. You must **log on** to the computer by using your name and password.
(   ) 9. Many **glamorous** movie stars come to the Tokyo International Film Festival every year.
(   ) 10. He's always **boast**ing about his new car.

---

a. very exciting and attractive
b. a brief written description that provides information about someone or something
c. to start the connection of a computer to the Internet or a computer system
d. to try very hard to do something that is difficult
e. to talk too proudly about something that you have done, or can do
f. to emphasize something or make it seem more important than it really is
g. the feeling of wanting to have what someone else has
h. to finally be in a particular place or situation
i. to leave out something, to not include something
j. a feeling of extreme unhappiness

III Getting the Gist (First Viewing) [DVD 01:54]

Watch the news and then choose the right word in each statement.

1. Looking at your friends' Facebook pages can sometimes make you feel (crazy / confused / envious).

2. Many people only put up something (positive / negative / unimportant) about them on Facebook.

Getting into Details (Second Viewing) [DVD 01:54]

Watch or listen to the news again. Fill in the blanks and choose T or F for each statement in the boxes.

How come ~?
どうして、なぜ

Chris Wragge: This you're gonna love in this morning's HealthWatch, Facebook **envy**. Have you ever looked at your friend's Facebook pages and wondered, "How come their ₁( ) and mine, well, not so much?" Well, you're not alone. As *Early Show* technology expert, Katie Linendoll now reports.

updates
更新された最新の情報

Katie Linendoll: Over the last five years, social networking sites like Facebook have become the place we ₂( ) publicly with family and friends. And more than 500 million user **profile**s are filled with images and updates of people enjoying the best moments of their lives.

Dana Welch (Facebook User): Everybody puts that they're going to Miami or they're doing fun stuff.

Comprehension Check

1. [T / F] Social networking sites like Facebook are becoming less popular.
2. [T / F] Some people get envious when they look at their friends' SNS profiles filled with enjoyable images.

Linendoll: However, a new study suggests that these sites could actually have a ₃( ) on your mood, and **end up** caus**ing** more **distress** than happiness.

put ~ on display
~を（サイトに）載せる

David Swanson (Psychologist): What you put on display is how great your life is, the cars you drive, the vacations you go on. Nobody's ₄( ) and so whenever you start to compare your life to those images, you're gonna be depressed, because you're gonna feel like your life is lacking.

lacking
不足している、十分でない

Brit Tashjian (Facebook User): The sad thing about Facebook is, you… you know, you'd never put up something like, oh, a big mistake I made today, or you know, you'd never put in the About Me section, you know, I'm **struggl**ing **with** self-approval.

self-approval
ありのままの自分で
よいと認めること

Comprehension Check

3. [T / F] Most people put up their mistakes or worries on their Facebook pages.
4. [T / F] Comparing your life with your friends' can make you feel depressed because it makes you think something is missing in your life.

Linendoll: Most of us tend to **play up** the positive aspects of our lives while **exclud**ing the negative. The result is that a Facebook profile never quite ₅(   ) and we end up comparing ourselves to a one-dimensional version of someone else's life.

one-dimensional version
一次元的な（表層的な）面

Alex Jordan (Psychologist, Dartmouth College): If we could overcome the need to compare ourselves to other people and the need to keep up with the Joneses, then maybe these effects I've described wouldn't exist.

keep up with the Joneses
隣人と張り合う

Linendoll: So just remember the next time you **log on** and get Facebook envy, the reality of one's life may not be as **glamorous** as ₆(   ) or **boast**s.

Katie Linendoll, CBS News, New York.

Comprehension Check

5. [T / F] People often put negative information about their lives on SNS pages.
6. [T / F] People's profiles on SNS pages may be different from their real lives.

Summary

Fill in the blanks with the appropriate words in the box below. Then listen and check your answers.

Have you ever felt ₁(　　　　) when you look at your friends' Facebook pages? You're not the only one. Social networking sites like Facebook are becoming more popular. People ₂(　　　　) their lives publicly with family and friends. More than 500 million user profiles hold the latest images and ₃(　　　　) of people enjoying their lives. However, a new study says that Facebook profiles end up causing more ₄(　　　　) than happiness. That's because most people play up the ₅(　　　　) aspects of their lives and exclude the negative. Then, when we ₆(　　　　) our lives to someone's Facebook profile, we become depressed. We feel our lives ₇(　　　　) what others have. Doctors say we must remember that the reality of our lives is not as ₈(　　　　) as a Facebook profile.

positive	lack	envy	distress
updates	share	glamorous	compare

Useful Tip

How come ~ ? と Why ~ ?

本文ではアンカーのクリスが **How come** their life is so perfect?（なぜ彼らの人生はそんなに完璧なの？）と言っていました。How come? はもともと **How** did it **come** about?（どうしてそのようなことが起きたのですか）を省略した形だと言われています。ここでは How come の後の語順に注意してください。疑問文なのに How come の後は主語＋動詞～？となっていて、通常の肯定文の順序になっています。疑問文のように主語の前に（助）動詞が来ることはありません。語順をあまり気にしなくていいので、使いやすい便利な表現です。同じ意味の Why を用いた場合には、語順が逆転します。

How come <u>you are</u> here?　/　**How come** <u>you know</u> so much about Japan?
Why <u>are you</u> here?　　　/　Why <u>do you know</u> so much about Japan?

VI. Conversation in Action

Put the Japanese statements into English. Then listen to check your answers.

Noah: Hey, Olivia. What's wrong? Computer problems again?

Olivia: Oh, it's nothing. I just ₁_____.
（フェイスブックにログインした）

Noah: Oh, I get it. You've got Facebook envy!

Olivia: What do you mean?

Noah: You know, when you check out your friends' profiles, you get depressed because ₂_____.
（彼らの人生が君のと比べてとてもすばらしく見えるから）

Olivia: Oh, you too? I thought it was just me!

Noah: Ha, no way! You just have to remember, ₃_____! Everyone plays up the good stuff, you know.
（だれの人生だってそれほど完璧じゃないってことさ）

Olivia: Yeah, you're right. Reality is ₄_____.
（彼らのフェイスブックページへの投稿ほど華やかではないわね）

VII. Critical Thinking

Discuss the following questions with your partner or group. Give reasons to support your opinions.

1. The news story says people often use their Facebook pages to play up the positive aspects of their lives while excluding the negative. What does that mean? Do you agree?

2. Do you agree that looking at other people's Facebook pages can make you feel jealous or depressed?

3. Do you have a Facebook page? Why/Why not?

What would you do?

1. Your friend has Facebook envy. He/She is depressed and says everyone else's life seems more interesting. What advice would you give him/her?

2. Someone you know tells you he/she wants to have a Facebook page, but doesn't know anything about it. How would you explain it and what advice would you give (him/her)?

UNIT 8

Smart Networking Tips

I Before You Watch

Look at the title and photos and then answer the questions.

1. What are the people in the photos doing?

2. What does the title mean?

II Word Match

Match each word or phrase with its definition below.

( ) 1. The results were **grim**. No one passed the test.
( ) 2. She did some **networking** at the career fair.
( ) 3. First, **identify** your errors, and then correct them.
( ) 4. I called the manager to **inquire** about the job opening.
( ) 5. My boss gave me a nice **compliment** yesterday.
( ) 6. He sent a **follow-up** email after the interview.
( ) 7. Teachers **utilize** several teaching methods to help students learn.
( ) 8. Please **stay in touch** and tell me how you are doing.
( ) 9. It's always important to maintain and **nurture** a good relationship with customers.

a. to find out who someone is or what something is
b. saying something good about someone
c. to use something effectively
d. meeting and talking to people to exchange information and advice, especially about business or career opportunities
e. to care for and protect someone or something so it will grow and develop
f. unpleasant or shocking to see or think about
g. something that continues or completes a process or activity
h. to ask someone for information about something
i. to continue to communicate with other people, especially by calling or texting

III Getting the Gist (First Viewing) [DVD 02:07]

Watch the news and then choose the right word in each statement.

1. Networking is very important to (keep / find / quit) a job.

2. (Avoiding / Using / Applying) social media is a useful way to make new connections or maintain close relationships with others.

IV Getting into Details (Second Viewing) [DVD 02:07]

Watch or listen to the news again. Fill in the blanks and choose T or F for each statement in the boxes.

Jill Schlesinger: The numbers are **grim**. Unemployment is 9.1 percent. And it's taking the average job seeker nine months ₁( ). That's why experts say **networking** is more important than ever before. Fifty-one percent of recent new hires landed their positions through networking.

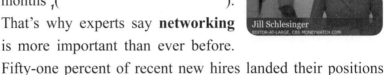

Many people say they don't like networking or they're bad at it. If you fall into this camp, there's some good news. Networking is ₂( ).

Michelle Tillis Lederman (President, Executive Essentials): Networking is really just another way of saying "making friends." And so every interaction you have is an opportunity to build your network.

Schlesinger: There's no right or wrong way to network. **Identify** how you best ₃( ) and then get to it. It helps to have a few conversation starters up your sleeve. **Inquir**ing about a person's job, asking their opinion or offering a **compliment** are all possibilities.

new hires 新規雇用者たち
landed their positions 職を得た
fall into this camp このグループに該当する

get to it 取りかかる、始める
have ~ up one's sleeve （手の内を見せないように）~を隠し持っている
conversation starter 会話のきっかけとなる話題

Comprehension Check

1. [T / F] Many people think they are good at networking.
2. [T / F] Asking someone about their job or giving them a compliment is a good networking technique.

Tillis Lederman: The most important thing in converting a conversation to a connection is the **follow-up**.

Schlesinger: Make a point to reach out within two weeks by sending a quick nice-to-meet-you email or an invitation to connect on LinkedIn. ₄( ) follow-ups can be equally

Make a point to reach out 必ず連絡を取るようにしなさい
LinkedIn ビジネス特化型SNS

effective.

Tillis Lederman: What are the things that you talked about, that you can just show them that you listened and you cared enough, to follow up on it. It could just be "Hey, how'd that birthday party go?"

to follow up on it
その後引き続きそれに対処するために

> **Comprehension Check**
> 3. [T / F] After you get to know someone, it is important to follow up by sending an email or link to a business SNS website.
> 4. [T / F] You can wait two months to send a follow-up email.

Schlesinger: Two more tips. First, if you have a job, don't forget to network internally. Introduce yourself to people in other departments. Second, **utilize** social media. LinkedIn is a good way to ₅(   ), and Facebook makes **stay**ing **in touch** with your existing network easier.

if you have a job
（すでに）仕事を持っていて（その勤め先の中で新しい仕事や部署を見つける場合には）

Man: I wanted to see if we were going to be able to get together this week…

Schlesinger: And ₆(   ) is key. You wanna have solid relationships in place before reaching out for help.

You wanna ~
～した方がよいでしょう

Tillis Lederman: You never know when you will need that network. And when you're constantly building and supporting and **nurtur**ing the network that you have, that network is going to be there when you need it.

Schlesinger: For CBS News, I'm Jill Schlesinger, CBS MoneyWatch.com.

> **Comprehension Check**
> 5. [T / F] Networking is not important if you already have a job.
> 6. [T / F] Using social media like LinkedIn is not a good way to make new connections.
> 7. [T / F] You should build and keep a good relationship with your network before asking for help.

V Summary

Fill in the blanks with the appropriate words in the box below. Then listen and check your answers.

Many people say they don't like ₁(　　　　) or can't do it well. But experts say it's an ₂(　　　　) way to find a job. In fact, networking is easier than you think. First, ₃(　　　　) how you best connect and interact with people. You should know some good conversation ₄(　　　　). Asking a person about their job, their opinion, or giving them a ₅(　　　　) are helpful examples. Next, ₆(　　　　) up a conversation by reaching out. You can send a nice-to-meet-you email. You can also invite them to connect on social ₇(　　　　), like LinkedIn or Facebook. If you already have a job, you should network with people in your company. And stay in ₈(　　　　). It's important to build and maintain a good relationship. Then you can ask for help when you need it.

media	compliment	follow	identify
important	networking	starters	touch

Useful Tip

want to = wanna =「〜したい」ばかりじゃない want の用法

本文では You wanna have solid relationships before 〜 とありましたが、この場合の wanna は「〜するのがよいですよ、〜した方がよいでしょう」という「提案」や「助言」の表現です。本文では親しみを込めて wanna とかなりカジュアルな言い方をしていますが、通常は丁寧表現の助動詞 may や might を使って、次のように用いられます。目上の人やお客様など、丁寧な言葉で接するべき人にも使えるので便利な表現です。

You **may** / **might want to** reconsider your plan.
（その計画については再考されてはいかがでしょうか）

人から You might want to 〜と言われたときは、アドバイスされているとのだと考えてください。

Unit 8 - Smart Networking Tips

VI. Conversation in Action

🎧 1-33

Put the Japanese statements into English. Then listen to check your answers.

Chen: Job-hunting is really tough!

Adam: Have you tried networking?

Chen: What's that?

Adam: It's talking ₁_____ or career advice.
（就職口のチャンスがあるかについて人々と話をすること）

Chen: Sounds hard.

Adam: Not really. First you ₂_____.
（会話を切り出す話題が必要なんだよ）

And then ask someone about their job or opinion about something.

Chen: OK. What's next?

Adam: Follow up by reaching out. I mean, ₃_____ or Facebook.
（メールかフェイスブックで連絡を取る）

Chen: Thanks. I'll give it a try!

VII. Critical Thinking

Discuss the following questions with your partner or group. Give reasons to support your opinions.

1. Why is networking important?

2. Give three examples of conversation starters.

3. Have you ever tried networking? Would you like to try it? Why/why not?

What would you do?

1. Your friend asks you for some networking tips. What advice would you give her/him?

2. You have been working in a company for several years. You would like to change your job, but not the company. What are some things you could do to network internally?

UNIT 9

Bringing Manufacturing Back to the U.S. via the Robot

I Before You Watch

Look at the title and photos and then answer the questions.

1. What does manufacturing mean?

2. What are some advantages of using robots in factories?

II. Word Match

Match each word or phrase with its definition below.

( ) 1. **Manufacturing** jobs will decrease if the economy gets worse.
( ) 2. She left the job because her work was too **repetitive**.
( ) 3. The coach thinks the team will **take to** the new uniforms.
( ) 4. The company president wants a **status** report from all the managers.
( ) 5. The fire caused a lot of **confusion**.
( ) 6. My brother studied computer **programming** at college.
( ) 7. Apple and Samsung are **cutting-edge** companies of the high tech industry.
( ) 8. Many people showed their **patriotism** at the Olympic Games.
( ) 9. Students must be **competitive** if they want to find a good job after graduation.

> a. newest and most advanced
> b. the current situation or condition of someone or something
> c. to like someone or something
> d. not understanding something, or not knowing what to do
> e. trying to be better or more successful than someone or something else
> f. making goods or materials in a factory
> g. loving your country and being proud of it
> h. repeating the same action over and over again for a long period of time
> i. the process or skill of writing programs for computers

III. Getting the Gist (First Viewing) [DVD 02:34]

Watch the news and then choose the right word in each statement.

1. The company is using a robot to (decrease / improve / reduce) productivity.

2. Using robot technology may (bring / find / stop) manufacturing jobs back to the U.S.

IV Getting into Details (Second Viewing) [DVD 02:34]

Watch or listen to the news again. Fill in the blanks and choose T or F for each statement in the boxes.

payroll processor ADP
米国の民間大手給与計算代行会社
Automatic **D**ata **P**rocessing, Inc.
(雇用に関する指標も提供している)

working an assembly line
流れ作業による組み立てラインを動かしている

Jeff Glor: The payroll processor ADP says private businesses added 166,000 new jobs in September. In the future, some of those could be **manufacturing** jobs ₁(   ) like China, thanks to a new piece of technology already working an assembly line in Pennsylvania. Here's Michelle Miller.

Michelle Miller: Meet Baxter. Just seven months on the line, he's the newest member of the team at Pennsylvania plastics manufacturer, Rodon.

Lowell Allen: He works 24 hours a day, 7 days a week, without a break.

VP
Vice-**P**resident
(副社長)

put ~ to work at …
～を…の仕事につかせた

Miller: Factory VP, Lowell Allen has put Baxter to work at ₂(   ): boring, **repetitive** jobs.

Allen: Our people have really **taken to** Baxter. He's non-threatening. He's… He's helping them do their job.

> **Comprehension Check**
> 1. [T / F] The robot at this factory is good at doing boring jobs.
> 2. [T / F] Workers at the company don't like the robot very much.

alongside ~
～のとなりで

Miller: Baxter is designed to work safely alongside humans. Six facial expressions communicate **status** to human partners — a raised eyebrow signals **confusion** if something's not right on the line. But most of the time, Baxter works alone.

Allen: And the best part I like is that Baxter doesn't ₃(   ). So Baxter doesn't talk.

Miller: Slow but steady, Baxter toils on 24/7 without breaks or benefits. He costs only $22,000. And even with power and **programming** costs, Baxter is a ₄(   ).

Allen: They do not necessarily replace anyone. In fact, we need to hire skilled people to maintain and program those pieces of equipment. They just enable jobs to be performed more efficiently and therefore less expensively.

> **Comprehension Check**
> 3. [T / F] The vice-president is happy about the robot because it works without any complaints.
> 4. [T / F] The robot costs more and produces less compared to human workers.

Miller: Baxter is part of the new factory floor — a **cutting-edge** mix of people and technology — that has helped to ₅(   ) enough to bring manufacturing back from China.

Hal Sirkin (Boston Consulting Group): So we're seeing now is companies bringing jobs back to the U.S. Not just because of **patriotism**, but because of pure economics. The wages are rising in China. The U.S. is getting more **competitive**. The average American worker is more than three times as productive as the average Chinese worker.

Miller: For Rodon and its sister company K'nex, that means 25 new jobs in three years.

Allen: We're adding equipment, people and possibly breaking ground next door.

Sirkin: Had the automation not been put in place for a lot of these companies, we would have ₆(   ) to the U.S.

Miller: Three to five million jobs are expected to be returning to the U.S. by the end of the decade. Michelle Miller, CBS News, New York.

> **Comprehension Check**
>
> 5. [T / F] American companies are trying to increase jobs in the U.S. just because they love their country.
> 6. [T / F] More manufacturing jobs will return to America because wages for Chinese workers are increasing.

V Summary

Fill in the blanks with the appropriate words in the box below. Then listen and check your answers.

Rodon is an American plastics ₁(   ). It's using robot technology on its assembly line. The robot's name is Baxter. He works 24 hours a day, 7 days a week without ₂(   ) or benefits. Baxter does boring, ₃(   ) jobs efficiently and more cheaply. He communicates by using six facial expressions. So it's easy for workers to notice when the robot has ₄(   ). Some workers might worry robots may ₅(   ) them. But using robots creates new jobs because people are needed to ₆(   ) and program them. American factory working conditions are changing. Automation is making the U.S. more ₇(   ). The cutting-edge mix of technology and humans is saving money and eventually bringing manufacturing jobs back from ₈(   ).

| replace | breaks | China | maintain |
| competitive | repetitive | manufacturer | trouble |

VI. Conversation in Action

 2-04

Put the Japanese statements into English. Then listen to check your answers.

Anna: Guess what! There's a ₁_____!
（私たちの組み立てラインにロボットがいるのよ）

Ryan: Uh, oh! Good-bye job!

Anna: No, it's not like that. The robot's name is Bob. He's going to do all the ₂_____.（退屈で繰り返しの多い仕事）

Ryan: Sounds good. What else?

Anna: Well, he works ₃_____.
（休みも給付金もなく一日中ずっと）

Ryan: Sweet! That should ₄_____. Well, time to go back to work.
（君の仕事が楽になるね）

Anna: Right. See you later.

Ryan: OK. Oh, and say hello to Bob!

VII. Critical Thinking

Discuss the following questions with your partner or group. Give reasons to support your opinions.

1. What are some advantages of using robots in the workplace?

2. What are some disadvantages of using robots in the workplace?

3. Can you give an example of how robots are used in your country?

What would you do?

1. How would you feel if you had to work with a robot? What would you like/dislike about it?

2. Imagine you had the ability to design and build a robot. What would it do? What name would you give it?

UNIT 10

Manners 101

I Before You Watch

Look at the title and photos and then answer the questions.

1. What do you think the title means?

2. Why are good manners important?

II. Word Match

Match each word or phrase with its definition below.

( ) 1. Harvard University accepts a lot of **bright** students.

( ) 2. Many **prospective employer**s will be at the Career Fair.

( ) 3. I'm not **familiar with** this area. Can you tell me where the train station is?

( ) 4. No **previous** experience is necessary for this job.

( ) 5. She got a **lousy** score on the test.

( ) 6. You can buy a good notebook computer for less than a **grand**.

( ) 7. I'm **head**ing **off to** the shopping mall. Do you want to come?

( ) 8. Figure skaters need a lot of **poise** when they perform.

( ) 9. My **superior** gave me a great evaluation. I'll be promoted soon.

> a. a thousand dollars
> b. existing or happening before now
> c. someone who has a higher rank or position than you, especially in a job
> d. intelligent and able to learn things quickly
> e. a company you might work for in the future
> f. to go in a certain direction or to another place
> g. very bad; not very good at doing something
> h. a graceful way of moving or standing, so that your body seems balanced
> i. having a good knowledge or understanding of something

III. Getting the Gist (First Viewing) [DVD 02:12]

Watch the news and then choose the right word in each statement.

1. Young people today know (a lot / much / little) about etiquette.

2. The news report says (popularity / position / success) in business depends on manners.

IV Getting into Details (Second Viewing) [DVD 02:12]

Watch or listen to the news again. Fill in the blanks and choose T or F for each statement in the boxes.

Cornell University
コーネル大学（ニューヨーク州イサカにあるアイビーリーグの名門大学）

Jim Axelrod: They are some of the nation's **bright**est, but Cornell University's engineering students still have a ₁(   ) (When we use a napkin,…) about etiquette.

After hearing from **prospective employer**s that today's graduates are about as **familiar with** table manners as ₂(   ), Cornell, like a lot of schools these days, brought in an expert. (Don't spit… no spitting into it…)

brought in
雇い入れた

Robert Shutt (Etiquette Trainer): Kids today, by… because of the conditions that they grow up in, haven't had as ₃(   ) as some **previous** generations.

Axelrod: You're trying to be polite and show etiquette, but what you're telling me is they're **lousy**.

Shutt: Well, I hate to use the word "lousy." They're just ₄(   ) often.

Comprehension Check

1. [T / F] Cornell students know more about typing than etiquette.
2. [T / F] The manner expert suggests that students have not been taught much about manners.

Axelrod: Of course, it's not just table manners. It's everything from what to wear to what you say. Meet Julie Fraser. How are you an exception?

flip-flops
ビーチサンダル

Julie Fraser: I think I have these dirty a** flip-flops on.

bleep
放送禁止用語をピーッという電子音で消す

Axelrod: We've been talking for five minutes and we have to bleep you. Don't you think there's a little something you need to learn about etiquette?

Fraser: I know. Probably.

Axelrod: But bad manners have meant good business for people like Robert Shutt.

Shutt: Research says that ₅(   ) of an individual's success in getting a job, keeping a job and getting promoted on a job are based on their interpersonal skills, and manners are part of your interpersonal skills.

Aemish Shah (a Cornell student): Eighty-five percent? That's huge! I mean, if you spent 40 **grand** a year, 20 grand a year on a ₆(   ), 120 grand and it comes down to you picking up your cup wrong or something.

Comprehension Check
3. [T / F] Teaching students manners is a good business for manner experts.
4. [T / F] Good manners are not an interpersonal skill.

Axelrod: That night Aemish Shah was just about to **head off to** his first college internship.

Shah: We do this in sequel?

Man: Right.

Axelrod: Today he's there. And while he hasn't exactly been picking up linen napkins,…

Axelrod: So, it's not like you're exactly eating at five-star restaurants.

Shah: We're not… We're not…

Axelrod: You're not worried about your salad fork…

Shah: No.

Axelrod: …he did pick up a notion during that etiquette dinner that he's brought with him to the ₇(   ).

Shah: Do you have the confidence, the **poise**, the etiquette to interact with **superior**s, to interact with someone above you?

Axelrod: Which is to say that even with an Ivy League education...

Shutt: Never talk with your mouth full.

Axelrod: ... ₈( ). Jim Axelrod, CBS News, Ithaca, New York.

Which is to say
それはつまり
Ivy League
北米北東部にある名門大学の総称

Comprehension Check

5. [T / F] The male student thought the etiquette dinner was not a good learning experience.
6. [T / F] Even graduates of Ivy League universities need to learn good manners to get a job and be successful.

V Summary 2-07

Fill in the blanks with the appropriate words in the box below. Then listen and check your answers.

We use interpersonal skills every day to communicate and ₁( ) with others. Having good ₂( ) is an important interpersonal skill. Many prospective employers complain that even bright college students have ₃( ) manners. So even if you spend several ₄( ) to attend a top university, you might not be able to get a job, keep a job or get ₅( ) on a job if you don't have good manners. Cornell University has started teaching manners to its students. Robert Shutt, an etiquette trainer, says the reason young people have bad manners is because they haven't learned as much about etiquette as ₆( ) generations. Aemish Shah is a student in the etiquette course. He says good manners will help him become ₇( ), poised, and able to interact well with his ₈( ).

| confident | superiors | manners | promoted |
| interact | previous | lousy | grand |

VI. Conversation in Action 2-08

Put the Japanese statements into English. Then listen to check your answers.

Risa: Hey, Minsoo. Don't you think there's a little ₁_____ about etiquette? （あなたが身につけておく必要があること）

Minsoo: Huh? What do you mean?

Risa: You sneezed and didn't cover your nose!

Minsoo: Oh, sorry. Does it bother you?

Risa: Well, yeah. It's not exactly a crime, but you're spreading germs all over the train!

Minsoo: OK. I'll ₂_____. And, Risa… （もっと気をつけるよ）

Risa: Yeah?

Minsoo: Could you turn the volume down on your headphones? It's really loud!

Risa: Oops, sorry! I guess ₃_____ ! （私たちマナーがひどいわね）

VII. Critical Thinking

Discuss the following questions with your partner or group. Give reasons to support your opinions.

1. Why is knowing about etiquette important?

2. Do you think etiquette should be taught to young people? By whom?

3. What are some examples of etiquette?

What would you do?

1. You are sitting on the train and the person next to you has bad manners: for example, putting on makeup, talking on the phone, talking loudly, etc. What would you do?

2. You are on a date with your boyfriend or girlfriend and you notice they have bad manners. Would you say anything to them? Would you continue the relationship?

UNIT 11

Baby Boomers Moving Back to Cities

I Before You Watch

Look at the title and photos and then answer the questions.

1. What does "baby boomer" mean?

2. Why do you think elderly people are moving back to cities?

II Word Match

Match each word or phrase with its definition below.

( ) 1. My brother is really **hip**. He has all the latest clothes and video games.

( ) 2. The government is preparing for a large **influx** of tourists for the World Cup.

( ) 3. Clean air, cheaper prices, and a natural environment are **benefit**s of living in the countryside.

( ) 4. I'm going to **retire** from my job next year.

( ) 5. The new subway line is **project**ed to be finished in five years.

( ) 6. He sold his old house because the **upkeep** was too expensive.

( ) 7. I don't have enough **disposable income**, so I can't go on a vacation.

( ) 8. New sports **facilities** are being built for the Olympic Games.

( ) 9. We had to **downsize** our staff from 60 to 25 people because of the poor economy.

---

a. the act or process of keeping something in good condition
b. a large number of people or things arriving at the same time
c. to make something smaller
d. a good or helpful result or effect
e. money that is left after paying food, housing, and taxes
f. to stop working because of old age, or you do not need or want to work anymore
g. fashionable, modern or trendy
h. to plan what the size, amount, or cost of something will be in the future
i. something such as a building or equipment that is built for a specific purpose

---

III Getting the Gist (First Viewing) [DVD 01:58]

Watch the news and then choose the right word or phrase in each statement.

1. Many baby boomers are moving from the (suburbs / cities) to the (suburbs / cities).

2. Some big cities are upgrading their facilities to attract elderly people who have a lot of (kids / housing space / money).

Getting into Details (Second Viewing) [DVD 01:58]

Watch or listen to the news again. Fill in the blanks and choose T or F for each statement in the boxes.

Greenwich Village
ニューヨーク市マンハッタン南西部にある芸術家・作家の多く住む区域で、現在はアーティスト系やストリート系の若者が多く集まる

A used to be the definition of B
昔はAと言えばBだった

Don Dahler: Greenwich Village in downtown Manhattan used to be the definition of young and **hip**. But the Village, and much of New York City, is seeing a demographic shift: an **influx** of baby boomers ₁( ).

69-year-old Jacqueline Carhartt.
What are the **benefit**s about living in the city when you **retire**?

Jacqueline Carhartt: Everything. Absolutely everything. We have the opera, music, theater. You can sit here, and look at the people walk by.

Comprehension Check

1. [T / F] Only a few baby boomers are moving into big cities like New York City.
2. [T / F] Boomers think they can do more interesting things in the city than in the country.

Real estate company
不動産会社

Dahler: In New York City, the elderly population is **project**ed to ₂( ) by 2030, and the trend is nationwide. Real estate company, Redfin analyzed the 50 largest cities from 2000 to 2010 and found all but 13 ₃( ) in baby boomers.

Dahler: With the kids gone, couples are questioning whether they need all that house, and all that yard, with all that **upkeep** they demand.

Dahler: Is this the death of the American Dream?

Leigh Gallagher: It's the ₄(　　　　　　) of the American Dream.

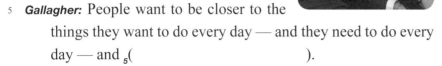

Dahler: Leigh Gallagher is the author of *The End of the Suburbs*.

Gallagher: People want to be closer to the things they want to do every day — and they need to do every day — and ₅(　　　　　　　　　).

Comprehension Check

3. [T / F] The number of boomer residents is increasing in 13 of the largest cities in the U.S.
4. [T / F] More and more boomers are moving into cities because they don't need their large houses and yards in the suburbs after their children move out of the house.
5. [T / F] Boomers want a more convenient life and want to be closer to other people.

Dahler: Within the next decade, retirees aged 65 and over will control 70 percent of the nation's **disposable income**. That has not gone unnoticed by cities. There's a full-out competition for those urban immigrants, and their dollars. Cities from Charlotte, North Carolina to Miami, Florida are upgrading public transportation and **facilities** to appeal to older residents.

Gallagher: It's being near activity, action, liveliness. It's a much more ₆(　　　　　　) of way of life, and I think that's what people want, especially after their kids are gone and, and moved out of the house.

Dahler: Retirees may have **downsize**d their ₇(　　　　　　), but they say they upgraded their lives.
Don Dahler, CBS News, New York.

Comprehension Check

6. [T / F] Within 10 years, younger people will have more disposable income than older ones.
7. [T / F] Some cities are upgrading public transportation and facilities to attract older people to urban areas so that they can live and spend money there.

retirees
退職者たち

not gone unnoticed
見過ごされることはない（必ず目に留まる）

full-out competition for ~
総力を挙げて～を手に入れようとする競争

action
元気や活力のある様子

Summary

Fill in the blanks with the appropriate words in the box below. Then listen and check your answers.

> Downtown New York City used to be a popular place for the young and ₁( ) to live, but not anymore. Many baby boomers are moving to the city after they ₂( ). The trend to live in ₃( ) areas is nationwide. After their children leave, many retired couples are wondering if they still need a big house in the ₄( ). A large house and yard need too much upkeep. The American Dream used to mean living in a big house outside the city. But now, many retirees want to be ₅( ) to things they want to do. For example, they want to go to concerts, theaters, or just be close to ₆( ). So, many cities are ₇( ) public transportation and facilities to attract elderly residents. They are expecting boomers to spend ₈( ) and improve the economy.

suburbs	closer	hip	money
people	urban	retire	upgrading

 With the kids gone （with ＋名詞＋過去分詞）の形

本文で With the kids gone,... という表現がありますが、この場合、with は「〜といっしょに」という意味ではありません。この with はその後に名詞と過去分詞が来て、「〜が…（という状態）なので」という意味になり、「理由」や「原因」を表します。つまり、「子どもたちが（成長して）家を出てしまったので」となります。with の後の名詞と過去分詞は「主語＋述語」の関係にあり、上記の例の場合には the kids are gone という関係が成立しています。
　　　　　　　　　（主語）　（述語）

With everything gone digital, school kids aren't required to learn good penmanship anymore.
(何もかもデジタル化したために、学校に通う子どもたちは、もはやあのすばらしいペン習字を学ぶ必要がなくなってしまった)

VI. Conversation in Action

🎧 2-12

Put the Japanese statements into English. Then listen to check your answers.

Max: I ₁can't wait to _____!
（引退して街に戻るのが待ち遠しい）

Ella: What? Leave the suburbs? Why? You have such a beautiful house!

Max: Yes, but ₂_____, it's too big. And the upkeep costs too much. （子どもたちも出て行ったし）

Ella: But what are the ₃_____?
（街に住むことの利点は）

Max: Absolutely everything! There's music, the theater. Well, even just ₄_____ _____ is relaxing. （人々が通り過ぎるのを見るだけでも）

Ella: You're right! The city is where the action is. I'm sure you'll like it!

VII. Critical Thinking

Discuss the following questions with your partner or group. Give reasons to support your opinions.

1. Why do you think elderly people want to live in the city after they retire?

2. Japan's elderly population (aged 65 or older), made up 20 percent of the nation's population in June 2006. Experts say it will increase to 38 percent by 2055. What do you think cities need to do to prepare for this increase? (e.g., government policies, work, lifestyle, healthcare, etc.)

What would you do?

1. What would be the best age to retire? Why?

2. Imagine you have worked for many years and are planning to retire. What would your ideal retirement be like? How would you spend your free time? Would you travel? What activities would you enjoy?

UNIT 12

Law Students Struggle to Find Work

I Before You Watch

Look at the title and photos and then answer the questions.

1. What are the people in the above photo doing?

2. Is it easy for law students in the U.S. to find jobs?

II Word Match

Match each word or phrase with its definition below.

(　) 1. The sales tax will **double** next year.

(　) 2. She is the **dean** of the English Department at my university.

(　) 3. He **land**ed a job with one of the top companies in Japan.

(　) 4. A **legal degree** might help you get a career in law and government.

(　) 5. I **assume**d you were busy because you didn't answer my text message.

(　) 6. This workshop will give children **hands-on** experience with computers.

(　) 7. Only **a handful of** people agreed with him.

(　) 8. We hope the meeting will have **tangible** results.

(　) 9. He just **drift**ed **into** that job. He isn't sure what he wants to do.

---

a. a small number of people or things

b. to think that something is true

c. to move slowly or change one place to another

d. actually doing something yourself, and not only studying about it or watching someone else do it

e. a person who is in charge of a department at a university

f. to succeed in getting something

g. a university qualification given to someone who successfully completes law school

h. real and not imaginary, able to be experienced

i. to become twice as big, twice as much, or twice as many

III Getting the Gist (First Viewing) [DVD 02:30]

Watch the news and then choose the right word in each statement.

1. Going to law school may not (keep / guarantee / seek) a full-time job as a lawyer.

2. To make students more competitive, a law school in California provides (high-tech / hands-on / impractical) training like internships.

Getting into Details (Second Viewing) [DVD 02:30]

Watch or listen to the news again. Fill in the blanks and choose T or F for each statement in the boxes.

Interest rates
金利

federally-subsidized Stafford Loans
連邦政府が助成する学生ローン（高等教育に寄与した上院議員のRobert Staffordが名称の由来）

Congress
アメリカ連邦議会

be headed to ~
~を目指す

Jeff Glor: The cost of a college education ₁( ) for many students tomorrow. Interest rates on new federally-subsidized Stafford Loans will **double** to 6.8 percent after Congress failed to extend them.

Whether you need a loan or not, if you're headed to law school, you may need to lower your employment expectations. Here's Carter Evans.

Comprehension Check

1. [T / F] The cost of a college education will increase because interest rates for college loans will go up.
2. [T / F] If you study at law school, your chances of getting a job after graduation are good.

Teacher #1: Let's turn and open our books.

Carter Evans: No matter how hard they study, half of these law students may ₂( ) as a full-time lawyer.

Frank Wu: There are too many law schools. There are too many law students. There are too many lawyers.

Evans: Frank Wu is the **dean** of the University of California Hastings in San Francisco.

Evans: I can't believe I'm hearing this from you.

Wu: We need lawyers. We just don't need that many.

class of 2012
2012年卒業組

Evans: Wu says law schools have overproduced lawyers for years. In 2012, there were 46,000 new law school graduates. But only ₃( ) **land**ed a full-time job that required a **legal degree**. For Hastings' class of 2012, it was 50 percent.

Wu: People rushed to law school because they thought… Well, this is a sure thing.

Evans: And whose fault was that, that their expectations were out of whack?

Wu: It just happened. Everyone just **assume**d that the economy would keep growing this way, that technology and outsourcing would ₄(   ). That's just not true.

Comprehension Check

3. [T / F] Only a little more than half of law school graduates could get a full-time legal job in 2012.
4. [T / F] There are not enough law schools and law students.

Teacher #2: With that as background…

Evans: To make its students more competitive, Hastings cut its entering class by almost ₅(   ). And it's replacing some classroom instruction with **hands-on** training. Peter Chau is one of **a handful of** students at a new criminal law internship program that will start this fall.

Peter Chau: Working in the district attorney's office will give me just a real **tangible** thing that I can really sink my teeth into, as opposed to just staring at a book.

Evans: Chau's internship guarantees a one-year job that pays ₆(   ). He will owe about 120,000 in student loans.

Chau: It is a large sum of money. But my education is worth it for me. That was my ticket out.

Evans: A very expensive ticket that Wu warns should be ₇(   ).

Wu: You shouldn't just **drift into** law school. Law school is not a backup. It's not a default.

Evans: And it may not be a path to a high-paying job or even one at all. Carter Evans, CBS News, San Francisco.

Comprehension Check

5. [T / F] UC Hastings is providing practical training like internship programs to their students.
6. [T / F] You should think carefully before you enter law school because you may not be able to get a high-paying job after graduation.

V Summary

Fill in the blanks with the appropriate words in the box below. Then listen and check your answers.

Many American college students get a government ₁(   ) to pay for their education. They pay back the loan after they graduate and find a job. But getting a job is becoming more ₂(   ) for law students. In 2012 only 56 percent of all law school students ₃(   ) a full-time job that required a ₄(   ) degree. Why? There are too many law schools. There are too many law students. There are too many lawyers. People chose law schools because they thought it was a ₅(   ) thing. To deal with this problem, some universities are ₆(   ) classroom instruction with hands-on training and internships. They hope this will help students get a ₇(   ). However, many law students will still ₈(   ) a lot of money after they graduate. Students should think carefully before they decide to study law.

| loan | legal | difficult | sure |
| owe | replacing | landed | job |

Unit 12 - Law Students Struggle to Find Work

VI. Conversation in Action

🎧 2-16

Put the Japanese statements into English. Then listen to check your answers.

Sofia: How's your job-hunting going?

Ben: Not real good. ₁<u>There were only</u> _____ listed at the Job Center. （ほんの一握りの仕事しかないね）

Sofia: The dean said we shouldn't assume ₂_____ just because we have a law degree. （私たちがよい仕事に就けると）

Ben: Yeah. What we really need is some ₃_____ before we graduate. （実践的な経験）

Sofia: I agree. But how?

Ben: A new ₄_____ is starting this fall. Maybe we should check it out. （就業体験のプログラム）

Sofia: Good idea! I'm sure that will help.

VII. Critical Thinking

Discuss the following questions with your partner or group. Give reasons to support your opinions.

1. Is working as a lawyer a popular career in Japan? What careers are popular in Japan?

2. Why did you choose your major? Do you think your major will help you find a good job after graduation?

3. How do most Japanese university students pay for their education?

What would you do?

1. You are a high school student thinking about entering a university. Think about your major and your career. You really want to be a (   ). But some people say it's difficult to find a job in that field. Would you change your major and career goal, or would you keep your dream?

2. You are studying in the business department of your university. You are a marketing major. You are having a hard time finding a job in marketing. A friend suggests that you take any job, even if it's not in your field. What would you do?

UNIT 13

Carbon Dioxide Making Oceans More Acidic

I Before You Watch

Look at the title and photos and then answer the questions.

1. What is carbon dioxide?

2. What do you think will happen if there is too much carbon dioxide in the ocean?

Unit 13 - Carbon Dioxide Making Oceans More Acidic

II Word Match

Match each word or phrase with its definition below.

(   ) 1. He made a **convincing** speech. Everyone agreed with his idea.

(   ) 2. Water boils at a **temperature** of 212 °F.

(   ) 3. The earth's **atmosphere** is affected by pollution.

(   ) 4. The level of **carbon dioxide** in the atmosphere has increased.

(   ) 5. A sponge **absorb**s water.

(   ) 6. The snowstorm **prevent**ed us **from** going to work this morning.

(   ) 7. Google and Yahoo! are internet **heavyweight**s.

(   ) 8. The police are **look**ing **into** the cause of the accident.

(   ) 9. Bring an umbrella **in case** it rains.

---

a. the air that surrounds the earth

b. to take in something, such as a liquid, slowly

c. a colorless, odorless gas, produced when animals breathe out or when carbon is burnt

d. to try to get information about something

e. to be ready for something that might happen

f. believable or true

g. someone or something of great importance or influence

h. a measurement that indicates how hot or cold something is

i. to stop something from happening

III Getting the Gist (First Viewing) [DVD 02:15]

Watch the news and then choose the right word or phrase in each statement.

1. The fishermen couldn't get enough young oysters because the oceans are becoming (colder / hotter / more acidic).

2. The oceans absorb (heat / seaweed / sand) caused by greenhouse gases and they keep the planet from overheating.

IV. Getting into Details (Second Viewing) [DVD 02:15]

Watch or listen to the news again. Fill in the blanks and choose T or F for each statement in the boxes.

Scott Perry: Scientists working with the United Nations said today that the evidence is more **convincing** than ever that humans are the $_1$(   ) of climate change. Surprisingly, their report indicates that the rise in air **temperature**s has slowed, but greenhouse gases are profoundly changing the oceans. Ben Tracy takes a look.

greenhouse gases
温室効果ガス（温室効果の原因となる二酸化炭素など）

profoundly
大いに

Comprehension Check

1. [T / F] Scientists claim that humans are mainly causing climate change.
2. [T / F] Their report shows that the air temperature is decreasing slowly.

Ben Tracy: This company near San Diego raises oysters. Last year, Dennis Peterson says they could only get a $_2$(   ) the young oysters or seed they need from hatcheries in the Pacific Northwest. It cost them about a million dollars in lost business. Why was it hard to get that seed? What happened?

hatcheries
孵化場

lost business
ビジネスにおける損害

Dennis Peterson: The oceans were $_3$(   ) as a by-product of increased CO_2 in the **atmosphere**.

as a by-product of ~
〜の副産物として

Tracy: About 70 percent of **carbon dioxide** produced on the planet stays in the atmosphere or is used by plants.

Thirty percent is **absorb**ed by the oceans, where it produces a weak acid. But it's $_4$(   ) to impact sea life and **prevent** oysters **from** creating their shells.

Comprehension Check

3. [T / F] The company got more young oysters last year because the oceans were less acidic.
4. [T / F] Carbon dioxide absorbed in the atmosphere has a strong impact on sea life.

Tracy: Carbon emissions also trap heat. Today's report shows oceans have absorbed 90 percent of that heat, raising ocean temperatures ₅( ). Had all that heat gone into the atmosphere, air temperatures could have risen by more than 200 degrees.

Lynne Talley (scientist): The ocean is really the **heavyweight** in the system. It is where most of the heat goes.

Tracy: Lynne Talley is a scientist with the Scripps Institution of Oceanography. She says oceans are ₆( ) from overheating, but sea levels are rising because the heat expands the water.

Talley: A lot of it's in the upper ocean, but there's a certain amount in the deep ocean… uh… and that's well away from the atmosphere. So you're moving heat all the way down into the ocean.

Tracy: Dennis Peterson worries about what that means for his oysters. When it comes to climate change, is the ₇( ) a canary in a coal mine?

Peterson: Yes, I would say it is. This is only the first thing we noticed.

Tracy: He's already **look**ing **into** expanding his other products, such as red seaweed, **in case** these oyster crates one day come up empty.
Ben Tracy, CBS News, Carlsbad, California.

Carbon emissions
炭酸ガスの放出
trap heat
熱を閉じ込める

Scripps Institution of Oceanography
スクリップス海洋学研究所

well away from ~
～からかなり離れた所に

When it comes to ~
～ということになると
canary in a coal mine
炭鉱のカナリア

red seaweed
《植物》紅藻（こうそう）食用となる
crates
枠の付いたカゴ

CBS NewsBreak 2

> **Comprehension Check**
>
> 5. [T / F] Because the oceans absorb a lot of heat, the air temperature doesn't increase much.
> 6. [T / F] Fewer oysters are the first warning sign that the oceans are getting more acidic and warmer.

V Summary

 2-19

Fill in the blanks with the appropriate words in the box below. Then listen and check your answers.

UN scientists are convinced that humans are the main ₁(   ) of climate change. Their report shows that the rise in air temperature has ₂(   ). However, greenhouse gases are having a big impact on the ₃(   ). Oceans are becoming more ₄(   ) because of the carbon dioxide in the water. The acid prevents oysters from creating their shells. Carbon emissions also trap ₅(   ). The heat is absorbed by the oceans. If the heat went into the air instead of the oceans, the air temperature would be much ₆(   ). Oceans keep the earth from overheating, but it also makes the sea level ₇(   ). The problem with oysters is the first warning sign like a ₈(   ) in the coal mine that tells us the oceans are getting more acidic and warmer.

| canary | heat | oceans | slowed |
| rise | acidic | cause | higher |

Unit 13 - Carbon Dioxide Making Oceans More Acidic

VI. Conversation in Action

🎧 2-20

Put the Japanese statements into English. Then listen to check your answers.

Nicole: Do you think ₁_____?
（気候変動は本当だと）

Akira: Well… yeah. Don't you?

Nicole: More than ever. I've heard on the news that oceans are ₂_____
_____. （地球が過熱するのを防いでくれている）

Akira: That's right. They absorb a lot of CO_2. Without them, ₃_____
_____. （気温はずっと高くなるだろう）

Nicole: Yeah. We really ₄_____ about climate change.
（何かする必要がある）

VII. Critical Thinking

Discuss the following questions with your partner or group. Give reasons to support your opinions.

1. Do you think the climate has been changing? Why/Why not?

2. Do you think humans are the main cause of climate change?

3. Give an example of how climate change has affected your environment.

What would you do?

1. You are a scientist who is studying climate change. What would you say to people who don't believe climate change is a problem?

2. What could you do in your daily life to help prevent climate change?

UNIT 14

"Technovation" Aims to Get More Women in the Tech Workforce

I Before You Watch

Look at the title and photos and then answer the questions.

1. What does STEM stand for?

2. Who has more careers in STEM, men or women?

Unit 14 - "Technovation" Aims to Get More Women in the Tech Workforce

II Word Match

Match each word or phrase with its definition below.

(　) 1. Women are trying to **break through** the glass ceiling in the workplace.

(　) 2. She is an **innovative** manager.

(　) 3. Scientists **figure** it will take a long time for Fukushima to recover.

(　) 4. Many people are **intimidated** by new technology.

(　) 5. Nobody likes to be **put down**. We should be polite to everyone.

(　) 6. He quit the job because he thinks washing dishes is **menial** work.

(　) 7. We can **make a** big **difference** in saving the environment by not using plastic shopping bags.

(　) 8. She wants to **pursue** a business career in New York City.

---

a. to force your way through something that is holding you back

b. nervous or frightened

c. boring, not important, requiring little skill, and having low value in society

d. to expect or think that something will happen

e. to have a good or important change or effect on something

f. to continue doing an activity or trying to achieve something over a long period of time

g. to say negative or insulting things about someone that makes them feel bad

h. using new and advanced methods or ideas

III Getting the Gist (First Viewing) [DVD 02:38]

Watch the news and then choose the right word or phrase in each statement.

1. There are (many / only a few / no) girls who are thinking of pursuing a career in technology.

2. This tech contest was held to (discourage / encourage / force) teenage girls to have a career in technology.

IV Getting into Details (Second Viewing) [DVD 02:38]

Watch or listen to the news again. Fill in the blanks and choose T or F for each statement in the boxes.

silicon-chip ceiling
「シリコンチップの天井」glass ceiling（出世を妨げる目に見えない障害）という表現があるが、ここではglassをsilicon-chipと言い換え、「テクノロジー分野における出世を妨げる目に見えない障壁」の意味

by design
意図的に、ある目的を持って

aerospace engineer
航空宇宙学の技術者

Jim Axelrod: While most jobs in technology are filled by men, you may be surprised by the size of the majority: 75 percent. To get more women **break**ing **through** the silicon-chip ceiling, a female scientist created a tech contest limited to teenage girls — ₁(   ). Here's Edward Lawrence.

Tara Chklovski: How can you change the world?

Edward Lawrence: It's called the "Technovation Challenge." One hundred teams looking at real-world problems and developing **innovative**, high-tech solutions. It's girls only — by design. Tara Chklovski helped create the contest, based in part on her own real-world experience.

Chklovski: I'm an aerospace engineer, and I have a degree in physics, and I was always ₂(   ) in that class.

Lawrence: In most schools today, she might still be. A recent survey found only 13 percent of high school girls — compared to 40 percent of boys — wanted careers in science, technology, engineering or math — STEM for short.

Chklovski: The problem is... is kind of deep. So a girl doesn't think that computer science or programming is ₃(   ).

Comprehension Check

1. [T / F] The majority of the workforce in technology is male.
2. [T / F] Many high school girls think computer science and programming are really cool.

Lawrence: The Technovation Challenge, she says, is designed to make it cool.

Chklovski: This kind of experience should be given to girls much earlier so that before they jump into the workforce, they have a ₄(   ) that says, "Yes, we can do this."

Lawrence: The challenge is bigger than a contest, of course, because smart teenage girls are all too aware of the latest headlines about rampant sexism in the tech world.
Here's what 16-year-old Claire Huang **figure**s she'd have to deal with if she chooses a career in technology.

Claire Huang: Not being **intimidated** by men in the workforce, not being **put down** by them, not being given **menial** tasks.

Lawrence: But she heard about the technology challenge, and she ₅(   ). Her team from Palo Alto's Castilleja High School reached the finals, developing an app that connects students with places to volunteer. (Very simple.) Claire's teammate, Mayuka Surukai, is now thinking about studying to be an engineer.

Mayuka Surukai: I'm really interested, in any way I can, just ₆(   ) in people's lives.

Comprehension Check

3. [T / F] The contest was designed to give teenage girls a positive experience of working with technology.
4. [T / F] Girls think that men and women are treated equally in the technology workplace.

Lawrence: The finals were held in California's Silicon Valley, and when that many girls get together in a place where boys get most of the jobs,…

Chklovski: Self-confidence dramatically increases. You have a lot of people ₇(   ). Um, it's a life-changing experience.

Lawrence: Claire's team didn't win. And it didn't seem to matter.

Huang: I'm not intimidated anymore. I'm ready to go out there, build our app, just **pursue** a career in this.

Lawrence: When she gets there, perhaps she'll no longer have to feel like a pioneer. Edward Lawrence, CBS News, Los Angeles.

go out there
今の状況に閉じこもっていないで、外に出る（行動に移す）

Comprehension Check

5. [T / F] The Castilleja High School girls were disappointed because they didn't win the finals.
6. [T / F] The tech contest gave the girls enough confidence to become engineers in the future.
7. [T / F] This news story suggests that more and more girls will try to have a career in technology.

V Summary   CD 2-23

Fill in the blanks with the appropriate words in the box below. Then listen and check your answers.

More men work in ₁(　　　　　) than women. Only 13 percent of high school girls want careers in STEM: science, technology, engineering, or math. A female engineer started a tech ₂(　　　　　) for high school girls. It's called the "Technovation Challenge." It aims to motivate girls to think about science ₃(　　　　　). One reason girls don't want careers in technology is the rampant ₄(　　　　　) in the workforce. They don't want to be put down or ₅(　　　　　) by men. They also don't want to do ₆(　　　　　) tasks. A Californian high school girls' team entered the contest. They made an app that connects students with places to ₇(　　　　　). The team didn't win, but they became more ₈(　　　　　) about pursuing a tech career.

menial	careers	confident	volunteer
contest	intimidated	sexism	technology

VI. Conversation in Action

Put the Japanese statements into English. Then listen to check your answers.

Heidi: Hey, Brad. I'm ₁_____ the Technovation Challenge.
（〜に応募するわ）

Brad: What's that?

Heidi: It's a tech contest. We think of innovative ways to ₂_____
_____. （現実の世界で起こっている問題を解決するための）

Brad: Cool! How do I apply?

Heidi: No way! It's girls only!

Brad: How come?

Heidi: Most ₃_____.（テクノロジーの仕事は男性によって占められている）We want to ₄_____
<u>stereotypes</u> in the workforce. （性差別的な固定概念を打ち砕く）

Brad: Sounds great! Go for it!

VII. Critical Thinking

Discuss the following questions with your partner or group. Give reasons to support your opinions.

1. Why do you think men have most of the jobs in technology?

2. How does the situation described in the news story compare to Japan? Do more Japanese men than women have careers in technology? How about other fields?

3. Have you ever had a life-changing experience? What happened? How did it change your life?

What would you do?

1. Your female friend is being intimidated by the male co-workers in her company. What advice would you give her?

2. What are some examples of sexism in Japanese society? (e.g., Education, lifestyle, workforce, media, etc.) What could people do to eliminate it?

UNIT 15

Flipped Classroom is Changing the Way Students Learn

I Before You Watch

Look at the title and photos and then answer the questions.

1. Who are the people in the photos and what are they doing?

2. What do you think "flipped classroom" means?

II. Word Match

Match each word or phrase with its definition below.

(　) 1. He made a lot of money by taking an old marketing idea and **flip**ping it.

(　) 2. My boss is eager to **embrace** the latest technology.

(　) 3. You need to **condense** your report to two pages.

(　) 4. I need more time to **digest** the new plan.

(　) 5. They **appli**ed new technology to the industry.

(　) 6. Can you **rewind** the DVD so we can watch that scene again?

(　) 7. She **synthesize**d old and new methods to make a new system.

(　) 8. The teacher **challenge**d her students to solve the problem.

> a. to make something such as a speech or essay shorter
> b. to make a recording (DVD, video, tape) move backwards
> c. to use an idea, method, etc. in a particular situation
> d. to combine ideas or things to make something new
> e. to eagerly accept something, such as a new belief or idea
> f. to test someone's skills and abilities
> g. to try to understand news, information, etc. especially when there is a lot of it or it is difficult to understand
> h. to do something in the opposite way

III. Getting the Gist (First Viewing) [DVD 03:22]

Watch the news and then choose the right word or phrase in each statement.

1. In a "flipped classroom," students watch lecture videos to learn the content outside the class, and the next day they apply the lesson (in the classroom / at home).

2. Students (like / don't like / don't care about) this new idea of learning.

3. In this new approach, (parents / students / teachers) can deal with different levels of students easily.

IV Getting into Details (Second Viewing) [DVD 03:22]

Watch or listen to the news again. Fill in the blanks and choose T or F for each statement in the boxes.

Jeff Glor: Finally tonight, a new way for school kids to do their homework. And perhaps a ₁(   ) for the parents who frequently get called upon to help. Dean Reynolds takes us inside the "**flip**ped classroom."

get called upon to help
手伝ってと呼ばれる、頼まれる

flipped classroom
反転授業

travel
（光や音が）伝わる、進む

Collin Black: The wave has to travel a lot farther.

Dean Reynolds: At Warren Township High School in Gurnee, Illinois, science teacher Collin Black helps kids ₂(   ) and sends his lectures home.

Teacher in video: Up down, up down, up down…

Reynolds: Black and others who have **embrace**d what's called, the "flipped classroom," **condense** their lectures into a brief homemade and often lighthearted video.

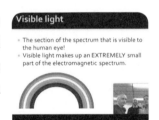

lighthearted
愉快で楽しい

electromagnetic spectrum
電磁スペクトル

Black: Visible light is actually the smallest, teeniest, tiniest part of the electromagnetic spectrum.

Reynolds: Students can **digest** the information outside of class whenever they like. The next day, they ₃(   ) and **apply** the lesson with the teacher in the room.

Comprehension Check

1. [T / F] Students watch the lecture videos at home or outside of class.
2. [T / F] Students use what they learn in the video with the teacher the next day in class.

Black: I can talk faster in the video, 'cause I don't have to slow down for the kids to make sure they're catching it, and…

Reynolds: Because they can pause…

Black: Right. They can pause it. They can **rewind** it. So I can talk faster and they can ₄(   ) quicker.

Reynolds: Freshman Hailey Dorsey echoed that point.

Hailey: We're able to, like, pause and then go back and, like, we… go over stuff that we don't really understand. The videos are nice. I actually like them. They're ₅(   ) than what we used to do last year.

echoed
同じことを述べた

go over stuff
事柄を何回も繰り返し学ぶ

Reynolds: Jared Cosey is another freshman.

Jared: It's really nice to go home, go look on the YouTube Channel, and you know, watch the videos.

Black: 'Cause you're moving slower,… (Thank you.) this… this is moving less.

Comprehension Check

3. [T / F] Students can pause or rewind the lecture video if they have trouble understanding it.
4. [T / F] Students don't enjoy learning in a flipped classroom.

Jon Bergman: The question I like to ask is ₆(   ) of your face-to-face class time.

Reynolds: Educator Jon Bergman, along with partner, Aaron Sams came up with the flipped classroom concept, originally designed for football players who missed class while on the road.

Bergman: We have school backwards. We're sending kids home ₇(   ). We send them home to apply, and analyze and **synthesize** content, and they can't do it.

face-to-face
対面の、直接顔を合わせての

while on the road
遠征中で

backwards
自然な流れに逆行して

Black: Perfect!

Bergman: And then when they come to the class, now in a flipped classroom, the difficult tasks — application, analysis and synthesis — happens [*sic*] ₈(   ) — the most important person, the teacher — present.

Reynolds: Three percent of teachers are flipping classrooms now. Eighteen percent have expressed interest, and 28 percent of school administrations want to do it.

Black: I can **challenge** the people who are doing really really well, and help the kids who really are struggling.

Was the amplitude lower, or was the amplitude greater, though?

No matter what, I would say, every day now, I talk to every kid.

Reynolds: For Collin Black, the flipped classroom is right side up,…

Student: The small one?

Black: When I see a kid who's been struggling and then they understand it. That's… that's what does it for me.

It can't be short and long at the same time, Danita!

Reynolds: …and for a whole group of young minds.

Black: Video for Monday!

Reynolds: Dean Reynolds, CBS News, Gurnee, Illinois.

Comprehension Check

5. [T / F] In a flipped classroom, students do the difficult tasks — application, analysis and synthesis — at home.
6. [T / F] This new teaching style is getting more and more attention from teachers and schools.
7. [T / F] Collin Black says that the flipped classroom makes it difficult to help students with different learning abilities.

Unit 15 - Flipped Classroom is Changing the Way Students Learn

Traditional: classroom → homework
Flipped: homework → classroom

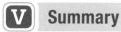 **Summary** 2-27

Fill in the blanks with the appropriate words in the box below. Then listen and check your answers.

The flipped classroom is a new ₁(　　　　) for teaching and learning. Traditionally students learn new things at school and do their ₂(　　　　) at home to review. But the new way is to "flip them around." Students watch the online lecture ₃(　　　　) teachers made at home or outside of class. The videos are helpful because students can ₄(　　　　) over stuff by pausing and rewinding it. The next day, the teacher helps them understand and ₅(　　　　) the lecture in class. More and more teachers and schools are getting ₆(　　　　) in this new idea. Students like it because lessons are much easier to understand. Teachers can ₇(　　　　) better students and help out students who are ₈(　　　　).

struggling	apply	go	challenge
concept	homework	videos	interested

VI. Conversation in Action

2-28

Put the Japanese statements into English. Then listen to check your answers.

Kou: Hey, Aya, we're going to have a flipped classroom this semester!

Aya: Flipped classroom? What's that?

Kou: It's a new way to do homework. The teacher puts ₁_____ and we watch it at home. （講義ビデオをネット上に）

Aya: Sounds awesome! We could watch it and ₂_____ _____, right? （好きな時に止めたり巻き戻したりする）

Kou: Yeah. And the next day we get to ask questions and ₃_____. （授業中にレッスンを応用する）

Aya: That sounds ₄_____. I can't wait to try it. （以前やったことよりもずっと簡単に）

VII. Critical Thinking

Discuss the following questions with your partner or group. Give reasons to support your opinions.

1. What does "flipped classroom" mean?

2. What advantages/disadvantages does this teaching style have?

3. Do you think students and teachers at your school would support the idea of a flipped classroom?

What would you do?

1. Would you like to try the flipped classroom at your school? Why/Why not? What course/subject would you choose?

2. You are a teacher and would like to use the flipped classroom in your school. What would you say to persuade other teachers and your students to accept this teaching style?

TEXT PRODUCTION STAFF

edited by 編集
Takashi Kudo 工藤 隆志

cover design by 表紙デザイン
Ruben Frosali ルーベン・フロサリ

text design by 本文デザイン
Ruben Frosali ルーベン・フロサリ

illustration by イラスト
Yoko Sekine 関根 庸子

CD PRODUCTION STAFF

recorded by 吹き込み者
Jack Merluzzi (AmE) ジャック・マルージ（アメリカ英語）
Rachel Walzer (AmE) レイチェル・ワルザー（アメリカ英語）

CBS NewsBreak 2
CBSニュースブレイク 2

2015年1月20日　初版発行
2023年3月15日　第9刷発行

編著者　熊井 信弘　Stephen Timson

発行者　佐野 英一郎

発行所　株式会社 成美堂
〒101-0052　東京都千代田区神田小川町3-22
TEL 03-3291-2261　FAX 03-3293-5490
https://www.seibido.co.jp

印刷・製本　三美印刷(株)

ISBN 978-4-7919-3388-4　　　　Printed in Japan

・落丁・乱丁本はお取り替えします。
・本書の無断複写は、著作権上の例外を除き著作権侵害となります。